CARTA'S HISTORICAL ATLAS OF JERUSALEM

An Illustrated Survey

Dan Bahat

Carta, Jerusalem

TABLE OF CONTENTS

Translated by Moshe Aumann
Cover illustration: Assaf Berg

ISBN 978-965-220-839-2

FOREWORD

Jerusalem is a symbol and a dream — the eternal capital of
Israel. But besides the heavenly Jerusalem, there are many more
Jerusalems. There is the Jerusalem of the ages: the historic city
of conquerors and kings, prophets, wise men, and story-tellers.

There is sacred Jerusalem, the Jerusalem of faith — the faith of
Israel, of Christianity, of Islam, and of their common and divergent
origins, their various sects and leaders.

And side by side with this, is the Jerusalem of stone and
mountain, layered with ancient sounds, colors and winds.

There is the Jerusalem of rapid creation and development, of
the effort to build a city of the future while guarding Jerusalem's
unique character and beauty, her message of tranquility and
peaceful coexistence.

The impressive extensive development of Jerusalem — reflected
in the building of new neighborhoods, the uncovering of historical
archaeological treasures, the careful preservation and renovation
of significant sites of all the eras — and the establishment
of scientific, social and cultural institutions — will oblige the
publishers to continually update future editions of this atlas for the
lovers of Jerusalem who, I am sure, will derive great pleasure and
much information from it.

It is a difficult task to portray Jerusalem through facts, figures and
maps, and I congratulate the initiators of this beautiful atlas.

Teddy Kollek
Mayor of Jerusalem

ANCIENT JERUSALEM: AN OVERVIEW

Jerusalem is situated in the heart of the Judean mountain range, on the crest of the ridge that forms the dividing tine between the Judean lowlands to the west and the Judean desert to the east. A hilltop city in ancient times could take advantage of its topographical setting if it was built in such a way that its outer walls rested on natural barriers — valleys, streams :and boulders encompassing the inhabited hilltops. So it was with Jerusalem from its inception; and it is this fact which in large measure has determined the city's area, its boundaries and the direction of its expansion down through the centuries.

The city had its beginnings on the hilltop known as the City of David. Later it expanded northward to embrace also the Temple Mount. In the course of time, Jerusalem continued to expand in the direction of Mount Zion and the hills to the west and north of the original city. All of these elevations are located in the area of the Kidron Valley drainage basin. Indeed, it is the course of the Kidron and that of the other streams draining into it that had a decisive influence on the fixing of the city's boundaries on all sides.

The source of the Kidron is to be found in a broad valley north of the Old City, not far from what is today the district of Meah She'arim. At this point it is called the Valley of Simon the Just and in Arabic Wadi el-Joz. From here the valley runs eastward and, a short distance further on, southward. This segment of the Kidron Valley separates the city from the long range comprised of Mount Scopus and the Mount of Olives which lies to the east. In this segment too we find the Kidron's only active spring, the Gihon, producing water the year round. It is near this spring, on the western bank of the Kidron Valley, that Jerusalem was established. The Kidron thus formed the city's eastern boundary from its very inception. In the Second Temple period it bounded the city to the north too, since the Third Wall was built in the vicinity of its first segment, the Valley of Simon the Just. South of Jerusalem, the Kidron continues its downward journey until it empties into the Dead Sea, some twenty miles to the southeast.

South of the hill that was the site of the original Jerusalem, the City of David, lies the Valley of Hinnom, a tributary to the Kidron Valley. The beginning of this valley is in western Jerusalem — in the vicinity of what is now known as France Square. From this point its direction is eastward to the approaches of the Jaffa Gate, and then southward around Mount Zion, and eastward until it merges with the Kidron Valley.

Until 1860, the Hinnom Valley marked the southern and southwestern boundaries of Jerusalem. In that year, Mishkenot Sha'ananim was built, becoming the first Jerusalem neighbourhood southwest of the Hinnom Valley, beyond the walls of Old Jerusalem.

Through the heart of the Old City runs the Tyropoeon Valley (erroneously translated 'Valley of the Cheesemakers'). This valley divides the city into an eastern and a western range. It originates in what is today the Morasha district, in northern Jerusalem, passes through the Damascus Gate, bisects the Old City from north to south along a street named after it, Rehov Hagai ('Street of the Valley' or in Arabic 'El-Wad'), leaves the Old City by way of the Dung Gate, along the Temple Mount and the City of David, and finally joins the Kidron Valley — a little to the north of its junction with the Valley of Hinnom.

The Tyropoeon Valley bounded the City of David on the west, and on it was to rest the Western Wall of the Temple Compound, as well as the western wall of the Antonia Fortress, just north of the Temple Compound. During the early history of Jerusalem, this

JERUSALEM 1917. Aerial view.

valley formed a natural barrier to westward expansion. Later, when the city did expand westward, a bridge spanned its width to provide a link between the eastern and western banks of the valley. The vestiges of this bridge — known as Wilson's Arch — now form part of the ceiling of a building that bounds the Western Wall Square on the north.

The Beth Zetha Valley (or St. Anne Valley) is the northernmost of the natural depressions that link up with the Kidron Valley. Originating in today's American Colony, in East Jerusalem, it runs into the Old City just west of the Rockefeller Museum, crosses the Moslem Quarter and enters the Kidron Valley at the foot of the northeastern corner of the Temple Mount. Just before that point it is joined, from the west, by a small depression that runs across the northern part of the Temple Mount.

It is the course of the Beth Zetha Valley that largely determined the northern boundary of the Temple Compound (and thus of the entire city) from the time of King Solomon until the erection, during the reign of King Agrippa, of the Third Wall, which traversed the Beth Zetha Valley. Notwithstanding its small size, this valley drew considerable quantities of rainwater, which accounts for the fact that we find here some of the more important of Jerusalem's water reservoirs, notably the Sheep's Pools, or Bethesda Pools, and the Pool of Israel (in Arabic: Birket Isra'in).

The western portion of the Old City is bisected by the Transversal Valley — the only one of Jerusalem's valleys to run from west to east (hence its name). Its course is from David's Tower to the Tyropoeon Valley, at Western Wall Square.

The watershed at which this valley begins is also the starting point of the short but deep Citadel Valley, which runs into the Hinnom Valley. In the Second Temple era, these two depressions marked the northern extent of the Upper City, and it is along their length that the northern wall of the city ran during that period of Israel's history. The point, on the watershed, at which these two valleys started out constituted a weak point in Jerusalem's defences. That is why King Herod fortified this corner of the city wall with three towers which he named Hippicus, Mariamme and Phasael.

Another valley which may have constrained the westward expansion of the city towards the end of the First Temple period was the depression running north-south through the Jewish Quarter of our day, along the Street of the Jews.

Not all of the valleys we have mentioned in this chapter are discernible today along their entire length. Certain sections have been filled in or levelled in the course of the centuries. Nevertheless, through measurements undertaken at various points of the distances from surface to bedrock, and on the basis of our knowledge of the city's past, it has been possible to trace the course taken by these valleys in ancient times with a fair degree of accuracy.

The pattern of hills and dales in ancient Jerusalem has enabled us to clarify a number of basic facts related to the history of the city. The Temple Mount and the Upper City enjoyed a natural system of defences on all sides. The same cannot be said, on the other hand, with regard to the elevations in the northwestern part of Jerusalem — the Beth Zetha Ridge, the Antonia Ridge and the North-west Ridge — all of which were largely exposed to any threat coming from the north. Attempts to fortify these weak spots in Jerusalem's defences were made artificially through the excavation of a system of ditches, or moats, along the northern portion of the city's perimeter, parts of which have been preserved to this day (alongside the road that follows the northern wall from Zahal Square to the Rockefeller Museum).

With an awareness of these elementary facts as background, we can better understand how Jerusalem was built and how it developed in the various periods of its existence.

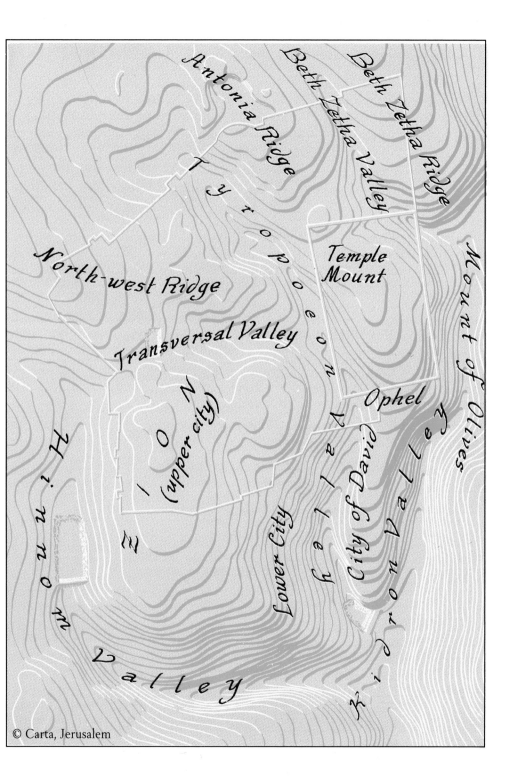

Antonia Ridge

Beth Zetha Valley

Beth Zetha Ridge

North-west Ridge

Temple Mount

Mount of Olives

T y r o p o e o n

Transversal Valley

Ophel

Z I O N (upper city)

H i n n o m

Lower City

Central Valley

City of David

Kidron Valley

Valley

© Carta, Jerusalem

EARLY HISTORY
UNTIL 586 BCE

TOMB OF PHARAOH'S DAUGHTER. Nobleman's grave of First Temple period, in Siloam. (Silwan) village; popularly known as the 'Tomb of Pharaoh's Daughter.'

The hill on which the city of David was built appears to have been inhabited since the Early Canaanite period. Evidence of this is to be found in the cluster of graves uncovered on its eastern slope. Other graves, discovered at the foot of the hill (in the village of Siloam, for example) belong to the first half of the Middle Canaanite period. No other traces., however, have as yet been found of human occupation dating to these periods in the history of Jerusalem.

The earliest remains of such occupation found here are from the second half of the Middle . Canaanite period: these are the vestiges of urban fortifications above the Gihon Spring. in the section of wall revealed by the excavations, the ruins of what seems like a fortified gate flanked by two towers were unearthed. Only one of these towers was found. This gate (?) remained intact for over a thousand years, until the destruction of Jerusalem in the days of King Zedekiah, in the sixth century BCE.

The existence of the city in the Late Canaanite period is attested to by the Bible as well as by a number of tombs from this era that were uncovered. At the end of this era, the Israelites decimated the Canaanite forces in the Ayalon Valley but did not capture Jerusalem. It was at this time that the Jebusites gained control of the city, and they held it until its conquest by King David some two hundred years later. Apparently of Hittite extraction, the Jebusites made an impact on the city that was to be felt for many generations.

The precise circumstances of the capture of Jerusalem by David are shrouded in mystery. The Bible tells the story in two versions — in the First Book of Samuel (5:4-9) and in the First Book of Chronicles (11:4-8). At first it was assumed that David captured Jerusalem by means of a ruse — penetrating the city's defences through an existing shaft, or water-pipe. Later it was discovered that the water supply system identified with this shaft was

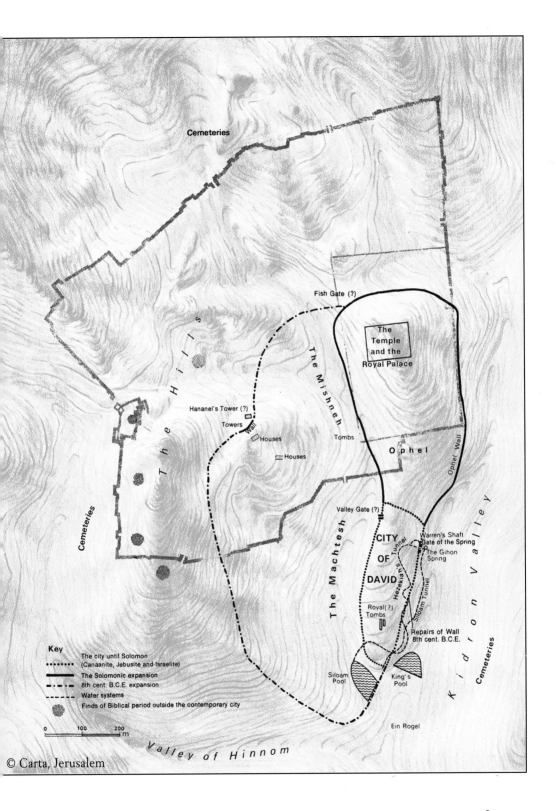

Cemeteries

Fish Gate (?)

The
Temple
and the
Royal Palace

The Hills

The Mishneh

Hananel's Tower (?)

Towers

Wall

Houses

Houses

Tombs

Ophel

Ophel Wall

Cemeteries

Valley Gate (?)

The Machtesh

CITY

OF

DAVID

Warren's Shaft
Gate of the Spring

Hezekiah's Tunnel

The Gihon
Spring

Siloam Tunnel

Royal (?)
Tombs

Repairs of Wall
8th cent. B.C.E.

Kidron Valley

Siloam
Pool

King's
Pool

Cemeteries

Ein Rogel

Key

- The city until Solomon
  (Canaanite, Jebusite and Israelite)
- The Solomonic expansion
- 8th cent. B.C.E. expansion
- Water systems
- Finds of Biblical period outside the contemporary city

0   100   200
                m

Valley of Hinnom

© Carta, Jerusalem

9

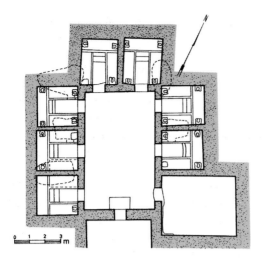

BURIAL CAVE OF FIRST TEMPLE PERIOD. Our knowledge on the expansion of Jerusalem 150 years before the destruction of the First Temple is based on excavations carried out in the city's burial-caves. Recently, a number of tombs were dated to the First Temple period, along with a cemetery located in the area north of Damascus Gate. The plan shows a burial-cave that was found in the courtyard of St. Etienne's Church on the Nablus Road. During the last decades a few noted scholars of Palestinian archaeology and history were buried here, among them F.M. Abel, L.H. Vincent and R. De Vaux. This is considered a typical First Temple burial-cave because of the following features: it is composed of separate rooms, wherein each room contains three ledges with a 'pillow' for the head of the deceased. This cave and a similar one found in the courtyard of the convent are two of the most splendid examples of burial-caves from this period.

actually built in a later period. It may be, therefore, that the 'shaft' or 'pipe' referred to in the description of the city's capture was a musical instrument (possibly referred to in Psalms 42:8). Jerusalem, in other words, like Jericho, may have been captured with the aid of a musical instrument. To counter this act of magic, Araunah, the Jebusite ruler of Jerusalem, also ventured into the metaphysical realm by putting the defence of the city in the hands of "the lame and the blind."

With the passage of time, and a succession of archaeological discoveries, we have been getting an increasingly clearer picture of the structure and extent of the city from the time of its capture by the Israelites and onward. Until a few years ago, research on this subject was based principally on descriptions found in the Book of Nehemiah. In the wake of Kathleen Kenyon's digs in the City of David, however, it became clear that the location of the city walls in Nehemiah's time was different from that in the First Temple period.

The most important source of our knowledge about Jerusalem in the days of the First Temple is of course the Bible — particularly the descriptions contained in the First Book of Kings and in the books of Isaiah, Jeremiah and other prophets. With the help of these descriptions and of archaeological findings, we may trace the development of Jerusalem in the First Temple period through three main stages. The city reached its greatest extent just before its conquest and destruction in 586 BCE.

In the first stage, in David's time, Jerusalem was confined to the hill known as the City of David. On the basis of the very thorough study carried out by Kathleen Kenyon in the 1960's in the area of the city's 'narrow waist,' it was determined that the northern fortifications of Jerusalem indeed passed through this area. (Although they were later destroyed without trace as a result of subsequent quarrying and construction work in the area).

It was in the same area that Macalister, working in the twenties, unearthed a city gate, (the Valley Gate in the accompanying map), which has not as yet been dated. Vestiges of the wall that encompassed the city in David's time were uncovered by Kathleen Kenyon above the Gihon Spring.

The second stage in the development of Jerusalem came during the reign of Solomon, who erected a large number of public buildings — pride of place being taken by the Temple and the Royal Palace adjacent to it. For this purpose, two areas were added to the north of the city: 1. the Temple Mount and 2. the Ophel area, between the City of David and the Temple Mount. A thick wall, a section of which was discovered in 1868 by the archaeologist Warren east of the Golden Gate, and a deep ditch at the northern end of the Temple Mount still discernible today between the Dome of the Rock and the ridge on which the Antonia Fortress was erected, apparently served to fortify this part of the city. Because of its location at the eastern edge of the city, the Temple Mount and its particular defence problems were from this time forward to play a weighty role in the defence of the city as a whole.

In a later era, King Herod was to erect all of the buildings he constructed on the Temple Mount on solid bedrock, replacing and erasing all traces of the buildings dating to the days of the First Temple. The end of the Solomonic era is said to have been the time of construction of the great water supply system named 'Warren's Shaft' after the archaeologist who discovered it. The purpose of the system was to provide an assured supply of water from the Gihon Spring to the city even under siege conditions. It was during the reign of King Hezekiah that Jerusalem reached the third stage of its development, conditioned largely by Assyrian military pressure on the surrounding area. Hezekiah's reign saw the fall of Samaria and the northern Kingdom of Israel to the Assyrians. Many of the inhabitants of that kingdom sought refuge in Jerusalem. Assyrian King Sennacherib's siege of the cities of Judah, the southern kingdom, reinforced the stream of refugees to the southern capital. The city, which in its existing dimensions could not absorb this large influx of newcomers, began to expand to the western slopes of the City of David, to the Tyropoeon Valley and even as far as the eastern slopes of Mount Zion. It was only some time later, however, that this new part of Jerusalem was fortified and a wall built around it. Wherever existing buildings interfered with the erection of the wall, these buildings were demolished to make room for the construction of the wall in its proper place (Isaiah 22:10).

It appears that the wall was built by Hezekiah in order to protect Jerusalem from the Assyrian King Sennacherib in 702 BCE. Hezekiah's most notable defence against the Assyrian troops was the hewing out of a tunnel between the Gihon Spring and Siloam Pool, which ensured a sufficient water supply to the besieged (II Kings 20:20; II Chronicles 32:2-8). This feat is noted in an inscription which was discovered inside the tunnel during the last century. (The inscription has since been transferred to the Archaeological Museum in Istanbul).

The geographical extent of the city in the First Temple period is also attested by the location of its cemeteries. Until a few years ago, the only known cemetery was the one found in the village of Siloam (Silwan), on the eastern side of the Kidron Valley, opposite the City of David. In recent years, however, additional tombs from the First Temple period were discovered in the excavations carried out by Professor Mazar southwest of the Temple Mount, and still more, dating to that period, were found near the Sultan's Pool and north of Damascus Gate. Judging from this wide dispersion of graves, Jerusalem must have expanded considerably in the two centuries that preceded the city's conquest and the destruction of the First Temple in 586 BCE.

TOMB INSCRIPTIONS from the end of the First Temple period discovered in the village of Siloam. Today, two are found in the British Museum whereas the third remains 'in situ.'

(Tomb) chamber in the slope of the rock (or tower).

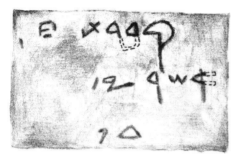

This is the tomb. . . . (cursed will be the one) who opens it.

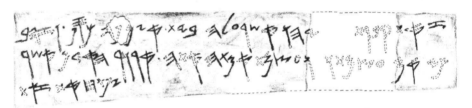

This is the tomb of. . . . Yahu who is over the house. There is no silver and no gold there, but the bones of his slave wife with him. Cursed be the man who will open this.

PART OF A STONE BALUSTRADE from below a window in the fortress-palace at Ramat Rahel. It provides evidence of the great importance of this building. Similar structures have only been found in royal palaces and it may therefore be assumed that this building was directly connected to one of the Judean Royal Families.

TOMB No. 7. Another view of the tomb showing the frontal access. The large archway leads to the larger, upper grave, and the small one, to the lower grave that was added later. A stairway led down to the lower grave. The wooden platform (cross-section shown in sketch spanning large archway) was composed of two segments: a straight upper segment, acting as floor for the passageway, and a supporting segment that was slightly arched.

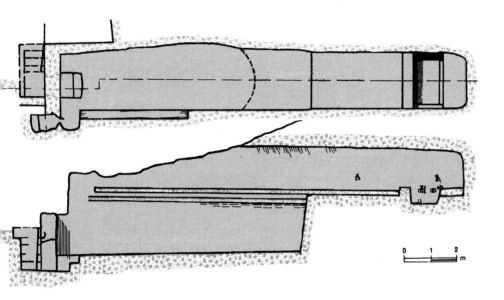

THE WEILL TOMBS. The excavations carried out by R. Weill in 1913-14 and 1923-24, on the City of David hill, are among the most important to be made in that area. Among other things, Weill discovered several burial-caves here that were broken into in the Roman period and their entire contents plundered. As a result it was difficult to ascertain their original purpose and who had been buried there; Weill, however, believes that these were the burial-places of the kings of the House of David. The top sketch shows a horizontal cross-section of Tomb No. 1 discovered by Weill. It consists of a passage about 16 metres long ending in a depression in which, presumably, the sarcophagus (stone burial casket) was placed. When the cemetery became overcrowded, an additional burial level was dug beneath the first one - as may be seen in the lower sketch, representing a vertical section. A wooden platform, constructed between the two levels, gave visitors access from the tomb entrance to the actual burial-place.

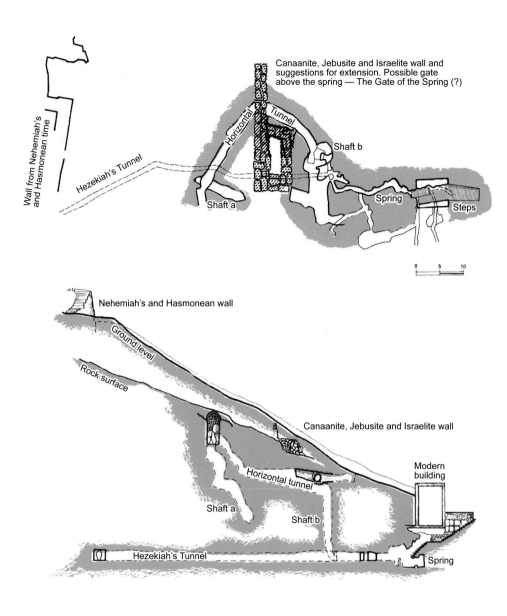

Canaanite, Jebusite and Israelite wall and suggestions for extension. Possible gate above the spring — The Gate of the Spring (?)

Horizontal Tunnel

Shaft b

Wall from Nehemiah's and Hasmonean time

Hezekiah's Tunnel

Shaft a

Spring

Steps

0   5   10

Nehemiah's and Hasmonean wall

Ground level

Rock surface

Canaanite, Jebusite and Israelite wall

Modern building

Horizontal tunnel

Shaft a

Shaft b

Hezekiah's Tunnel

Spring

'WARREN'S SHAFT.' This is the last vestige of one of the most ancient water supply systems in Jerusalem. The shaft is named 'Warren's Shaft' after the archaeologist who discovered it. The system is believed to have been created in the period of the Kings of Judah to enable Jerusalemites to draw water (unnoticed by a besieging foe) from a hidden spring, the Gihon) located outside the city wall. The two sketches above (one a plan, the other a cross-section) will give us a better idea of this system. A narrow shaft descends from the surface, within the city wall, to a passage with steps to a second shaft and from there through a nearby horizontal tunnel to the spring outside the wall. The sketches also show the discoveries made by Kathleen Kenyon in her series of excavations in the years 1960-1968. The main purpose of her dig was to uncover the walls that encompassed the city in the First Temple period, along the slope of the hill leading down into the Kidron Valley. The wall shown on the crest of the hill was built by Nehemiah in the Persian period and was refortified by the Hasmonean kings some 400 years later. This wall remained standing until the destruction of the Second Temple in 70 CE.

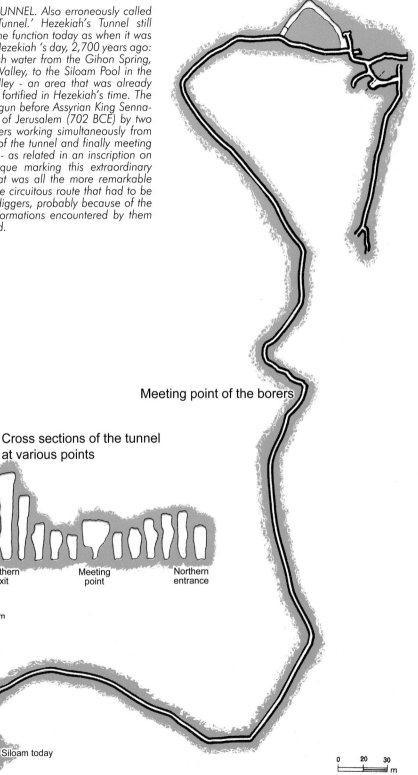

HEZEKIAH'S TUNNEL. Also erroneously called the 'Siloam Tunnel.' Hezekiah's Tunnel still serves the same function today as when it was excavated in Hezekiah 's day, 2,700 years ago: it conveys fresh water from the Gihon Spring, in the Kidron Valley, to the Siloam Pool in the Tyropoeon Valley - an area that was already inhabited and fortified in Hezekiah's time. The tunnel was begun before Assyrian King Sennacherib's siege of Jerusalem (702 BCE) by two teams of hewers working simultaneously from the two ends of the tunnel and finally meeting in the middle - as related in an inscription on a special plaque marking this extraordinary event. The feat was all the more remarkable considering the circuitous route that had to be taken by the diggers, probably because of the various rock formations encountered by them as they worked.

Meeting point of the borers

Cross sections of the tunnel at various points

Southern exit

Meeting point

Northern entrance

0 1 2
m

Pool of Siloam today

0   20   30
m

THE SECOND TEMPLE PERIOD
538 BCE - 70 CE

This period, which lasted about 600 years (from the Proclamation of Cyrus to the Destruction of the Second Temple) may be divided into three subdivisions: the Days of Nehemiah; the Early Hasmoneans; and the Great Hasmonean Kings.

The Days of Nehemiah

Until the arrival of Nehemiah in Jerusalem in 445 BCE, the city had remained largely in ruins, with only occasional and sporadic attempts at reconstruction being made by the few inhabitants who had remained after the city's destruction by the Babylonians. "The city, the place where my fathers are buried, lies waste, its gates consumed by fire," Nehemiah tells the Persian king, requesting his permission to leave Persia and go to Jerusalem in order to build it up again (Neh. 2:3). The Book of Nehemiah goes on to relate how the walls of Jerusalem were rebuilt, Nehemiah's nocturnal inspection of the city wall (Neh. 2:12-15), the work of reconstruction (Neh. 3) and the two thanksgiving processions that were held when the task had been completed (Neh. 12:31-41).

What may be learned from these descriptions in the Bible, as well as from archaeological finds, is that the dimensions of the Jerusalem of Nehemiah were the smallest since King Solomon had added the Temple Mount to the City of David some 500 years earlier. Nehemiah himself describes the condition of the city in these words (Neh. 7:4): "Now the city was wide and large, but the people were few therein, and the houses were not built." Nehemiah erected the wall on the crest of the City of David and thus greatly diminished the walled area of the city. At the same time, the boundaries of the Temple Mount most likely remained as they had been in the days of the First Temple, although the Jews' capacity for control of the area had been vastly reduced.

Basing ourselves once again on the biblical description and on the rather scant evidence uncovered so far by archaeologists, we may list a few of the sites that were included within Nehemiah's walls: the remains of the towers unearthed in the excavations of Macalister and Duncan (and erroneously attributed to an earlier period); the Water Gate (Neh. 3:26),

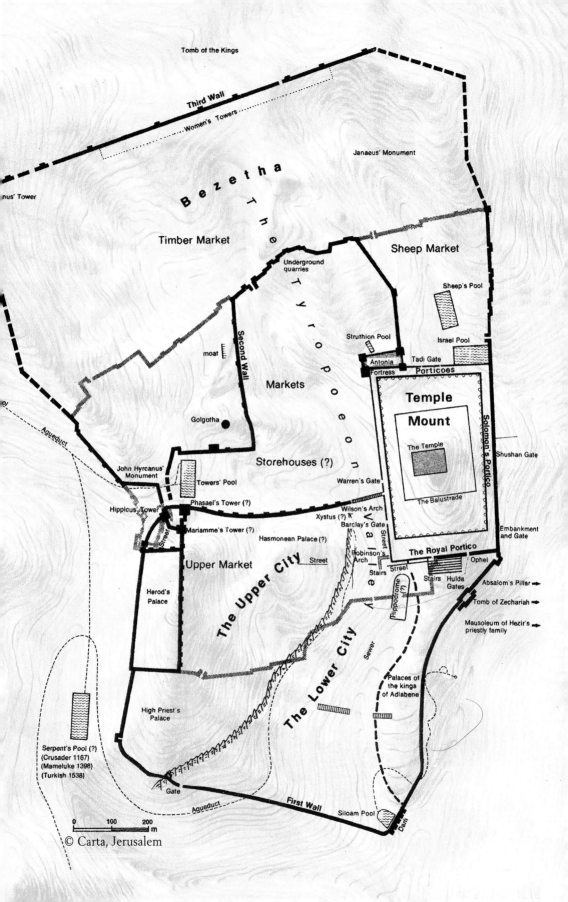

Tomb of the Kings

Third Wall

Women's Towers

Janaeus' Monument

nus' Tower

B e z e t h a

The

Timber Market

T
y
r
o
p
o
e
o
n

Sheep Market

Underground
quarries

Sheep's Pool

Struthion Pool

Israel Pool

Second Wall

moat

Antonia
Fortress

Tadi Gate

Porticoes

Markets

Temple

Mount

The Temple

Solomon's Portico

Shushan Gate

Golgotha

Storehouses (?)

Warren's Gate

The Balustrade

John Hyrcanus'
Monument

Towers' Pool

Aqueduct

Hippicus' Tower

Phasael's Tower (?)

Wilson's Arch

Xystus (?)

Barclay's Gate

Embankment
and Gate

Mariamme's Tower (?)

Hasmonean Palace (?)

Street

Robinson's
Arch

The Royal Portico

Ophel

Upper Market

Street

Stairs

Street

Stairs

Hulda
Gates

Absalom's Pillar →

Herod's
Palace

The Upper City

T
y
r
o
p
o
e
o
n

V
a
l
l
e
y

Hippodrome
(?)

Tomb of Zechariah →

Mausoleum of Hezir's
priestly family →

Sewer

The Lower City

Palaces of
the kings
of Adiabene

High Priest's
Palace

Serpent's Pool (?)
(Crusader 1167)
(Mameluke 1398)
(Turkish 1538)

Gate

0   100   200
m

Aqueduct

First Wall

Siloam Pool

Dam

© Carta, Jerusalem

HERODIAN WALL. Section of the Herodian eastern wall of the Temple Mount. Note the vertical 'seam' between parts of the wall representing different construction styles, and the vestiges of an ancient bridge and gate (of uncertain purpose).

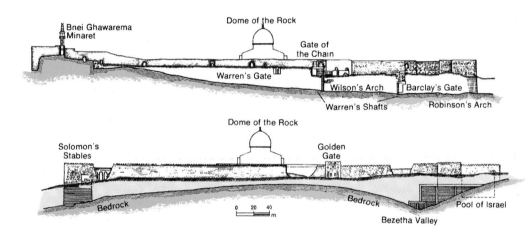

THE TEMPLE MOUNT IN HEROD'S DAY. King Herod's construction projects on the Temple Mount are reckoned among the grandest in the history of the Roman Empire. To create the huge platform that was necessary for the construction of the Temple Compound, Herod had a terrace built around the hill which in some places reached a height of 50 metres. It was also necessary, for this purpose, partly to block up the Tyropoeon and Bezetha Valleys which flanked the Temple Mount on its western and northern sides. The above sketches depict the walls of the Temple Mount in cross-section, looking from the west (upper sketch) and from the east (lower).

located apparently near the Siloam Pool (which had served since King Hezekiah's time as Jerusalem's main source of water as the Gihon Spring had apparently been covered over and forgotten about at that time); and finally the Wide Wall, traces of which were found by Prof. Nahman Avigad during his excavations in the Jewish Quarter of the Old City and which, by the biblical account, ran adjacent to Nehemiah's wall and abutted it at one point at least.

These details, together with the names of other known places mentioned in the third chapter of the Book of Nehemiah, in which the construction of the wall is described in detail, have enabled us to trace the general course of the walls of Jerusalem in the days of Nehemiah.

Hasmonean Rule

At the time of the outbreak of the Hasmonean revolt, Jerusalem was still the same small size it had been since the days of Nehemiah. From the archaeological finds on the hill of the City of David, it transpires that Hellenistic culture had not penetrated Jerusalem as it had the other Judean cities. Thus it may be surmised that Jerusalem remained as it had been throughout the Ptolemaic period (333-198 BCE). Such penetration did take place, however, somewhat later as a result of internal squabbles among various groups vying with each other — as we are told in the Book of the Maccabees — for control of the city. Our picture of the geographical extent and the buildings of Jerusalem in this period is not complete. According to the Second Book of the Maccabees (4:7-17), Jerusalem, like other cities within the Seleucid realm, was turned into a Hellenistic city, with recognized Hellenistic institutions such as a gymnasium, an ephebeon (young citizens' academy), a boule (town council), a temple to the city god and the like. Much effort has been invested in trying to uncover traces of these buildings, as well as of other edifices mentioned in our sources, such as the fortress built for his garrison troops by Bacchides in Jerusalem (I Maccabees 1:29-30). However, nothing has been found to date.

Archaeological excavations and studies conducted in the Upper City (encompassing today the Jewish and Armenian Quarters and Mount Zion) indicate that this area was largely inhabited during the Maccabean period. One should therefore look for Maccabean Jerusalem in the original City of David. The city's citadel, the Acra, which archaeologists have been seeking in the area of the Jewish Quarter, should perhaps be sought at the southeastern corner of the Temple Mount. Kathleen Kenyon believed the Maccabean city to have extended over that portion of the Tyropoeon Valley that was included in the City of David.

INSCRIPTION discovered in 1931 among the treasures of the Russian Church on the summit of the Mount of Olives. It reads, "Hither were brought the bones of Uzziah, King of Judah — do not open." It is apparently a tombstone from the secondary burial of Uzziah. The original site of burial is unknown as also are the reasons for the transfer of his body.

The Hasmonean Kings and the House of Herod

It was in this period, beginning with King Alexander Janneus and ending with the destruction of the Second Temple, that Jerusalem reached the peak of its glory, as reported in various contemporary descriptions, particularly that of Josephus Flavius. What is known to us today about the map of Jerusalem in that period is based mainly on Josephus' detailed descriptions of the siege of the city by the Romans and of the battles between Jews and Romans (*The Jewish War*, Books V and VI), as well as on his earlier descriptions (Antiquities of the Jews, XV, 1; *The Jewish War*, I, 21:1). Much additional information about the period has been gained in the wake of the archaeological work done in Jerusalem which took on entirely new dimensions after the 1967 Six-Day War.

The heyday of the Hasmonean dynasty was the period in which Jerusalem began to spill over beyond the confines of the City of David, its historic nucleus. With the rise of the great kings of the Hasmonean dynasty, the city expanded in the direction of the Tyropoeon Valley and of Mount Zion, thus forming the Upper City, which was eventually to become the hub of Jerusalem. In the reign of Alexander Janneus (early first century BCE) the Upper City was bounded on the north and the west by a wall whose remains still exist today. On the south and the east, the Upper City was protected by a massive escarpment dropping into the Hinnom and Tyropoeon Valleys. (Part of this escarpment is still visible beneath the houses resting on the eastern edge of the Jewish Quarter, opposite today's Western Wall esplanade). Another wall section was built later, extending from the southern slope of Mount Zion to the Siloam Pool. This section, traces of which were discovered in the last century, was built in stages that are difficult to date with any accuracy. It is certain, however, that it was built by the Hasmoneans. On the eastern side, from the Siloam Pool northward, the wall (first built by Nehemiah) of the City of David

MONUMENTAL INSCRIPTION, broken in two pieces, found near the Temple Mount. The first was discovered around 1850 and is today in Paris: the second was found during the Western Wall excavations in 1973. Apparently the inscription marked the place where the city elders were to be seated during ceremonies held in front of the Temple Mount. Or possibly it marked the site of some institution connected with the Temple Mount.

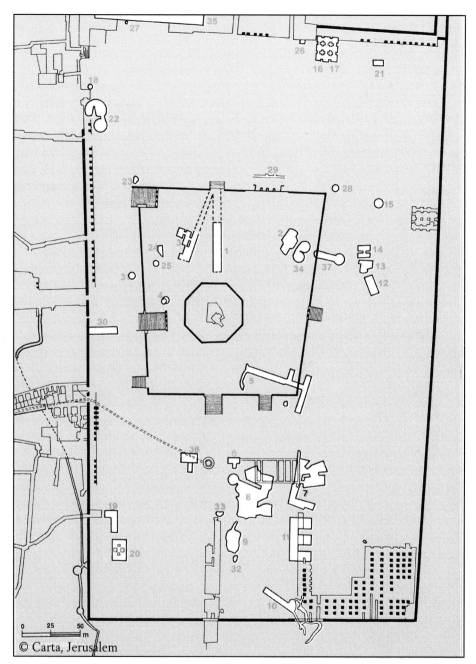

WATERWORKS ON THE TEMPLE MOUNT. A complex system of waterworks had to be provided to meet the large water requirements of the Temple. When the terrace was built and filled in to create the platform for the construction of the Temple, a large number of depressions had been left in the mass to serve as water reservoirs. Presumably, additional cisterns were dug there in later periods, but this is difficult to substantiate because very little has been done to investigate the matter since Warren's survey of the last century. The locations and approximate shapes of the cisterns are indicated in the above sketch. Of special interest are cisterns No. 19, 20 and 30, which served originally (in the Second Temple period) as entrance passages to the Temple Mount and were later sealed and used as cisterns. Possibly, cisterns No. 1 and 3 similarly served at first as Temple exits for the priests.

21

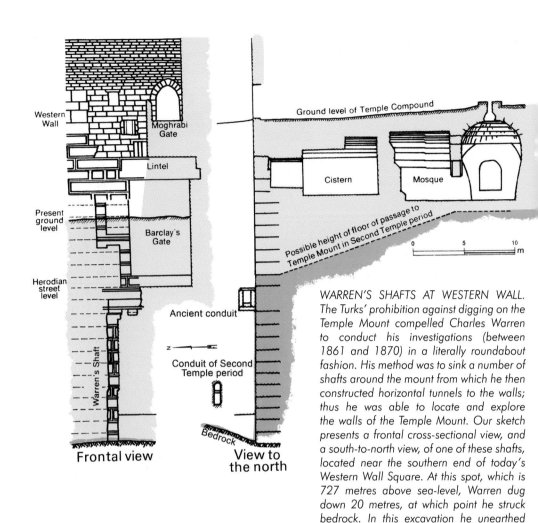

Western Wall

Moghrabi Gate

Lintel

Present ground level

Barclay's Gate

Herodian street level

Ancient conduit

Warren's Shaft

Conduit of Second Temple period

Bedrock

Frontal view

View to the north

Ground level of Temple Compound

Cistern

Mosque

Possible height of floor of passage to Temple Mount in Second Temple period

0   5   10
m

WARREN'S SHAFTS AT WESTERN WALL. The Turks' prohibition against digging on the Temple Mount compelled Charles Warren to conduct his investigations (between 1861 and 1870) in a literally roundabout fashion. His method was to sink a number of shafts around the mount from which he then constructed horizontal tunnels to the walls; thus he was able to locate and explore the walls of the Temple Mount. Our sketch presents a frontal cross-sectional view, and a south-to-north view, of one of these shafts, located near the southern end of today's Western Wall Square. At this spot, which is 727 metres above sea-level, Warren dug down 20 metres, at which point he struck bedrock. In this excavation he unearthed Barclay's Gate, which had been discovered some years previously and whose lintel can be seen today at the southern end of the Western Wall. Above Barclay's Gate is the Mughrabi Gate, today the entrance to the Temple Mount from the Western Wall Square.

0   5   10
m

SECTION OF THIRD WALL. While the general course of the Third Wall has been known for many years, it is only now, with the improvement of methods of archaeological dating, that it has become possible to date the construction of this wall with greater precision and to determine its exact position. The discovery that this wall had already been in place in the first century has finally settled a long-standing dispute among scholars on the location and role of the Third Wall in the defence of Jerusalem during the Second Temple era.

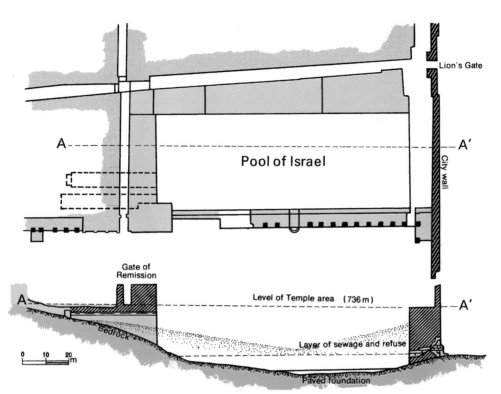

Pool of Israel

Lion's Gate

City wall

A --- --- A'

Gate of
Remission

A --- Level of Temple area (736 m) --- A'

Bedrock

Layer of sewage and refuse

Paved foundation

0 10 20 m

THE BEZETHA BROOK. This brook which in ancient times served as one of Jerusalem's most important sources of water had its lower section filled in when the Temple Mount platform was built. Certain sections of it were walled up to form pools, the best known being the Sheep's Pools and the Pool of Israel. The top sketch shows a bird's eye view of the Pool of Israel, the city's largest, and the bottom one — a vertical cross-section. The name of this pool is derived from the Arabic Birket Isra'in; its ancient name is not known. It was 110 metres long, 39 wide and 27 deep, with a capacity of some 100,000 cubic metres. In 1934 it was filled in because the water had become a health hazard.

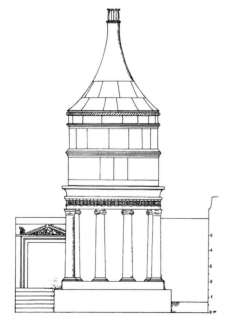

THE TOMB OF ABSALOM. The three monuments in the Kidron Valley, opposite the southeastern corner of the Temple Mount, were all built by wealthy citizens of Jerusalem in the Second Temple period. Of the three, only the tomb of the priestly family of Hezir has been positively identified as the actual tomb of that family, thanks to an ancient inscription preserved on the monument to this day. The most elaborate and impressive one is that known as 'Absalom's Tomb,' built in the Herodian period. In its lower part, hewn out of rock, was the burial chamber, atop which the cone-shaped memorial itself was constructed. In the course of time, this fine-looking tomb came to be associated with various notables such as the kings of the House of David. In the last few centuries it has been popularly identified with Absalom, son of King David; this attribution, however, is quite unfounded.

23

VIEW FROM THE TEMPLE MOUNT. This view takes in the area where the Antonia Fortress once stood. Beneath the new buildings in the background, signs are clearly visible of stonecutting done for the Temple Mount platform which required levelling part of Antonia hill.

continued to serve its defensive function until Jerusalem was destroyed by the Romans in the year 70 CE. In the writings of Josephus Flavius, this wall, in its entirety, is known as the First Wall. Almost along its entire length, this wall rested on the sides of the valleys that encompass the city. It had a number of gates, only one of which has so far been uncovered on Mount Zion.

As the city continued to expand northward, a new wall was erected, apparently by King Herod. Josephus refers to this edifice as the Second Wall. Except for some evidence of it at the Damascus Gate, and possibly some found in the Russian Church near the Church of the Holy Sepulchre, no traces have yet been found of this wall which is described only briefly by Josephus. Thus the Second Wall extended to the Antonia Fortress (north of the Temple Mount) in the east, and to the Genneth Gate in the west. The precise location of this gate has so far not been identified, but presumably it was in the vicinity of what is known today as David's Tower. Again following Josephus' description and the few vestiges of this wall, it may be surmised that it passed through today's Muristan area, along the present street of Khan ez-Zeit, up to the Damascus Gate, thence along today's northern wall approximately to Herod's Gate and back again to the Antonia Fortress. The area bounded by this new wall included residential zones as well as public storehouses. The wall bounded the midsection of the Tyropoeon Valley, which offered access to the Temple Mount (through Warren Gate), and the Antonia Fortress. Structural remains (no longer visible because they have been covered) found near the western tower of Damascus Gate indicate that this was the site of one of the gates in the Second Wall. A cave-tomb dating to the Second Temple period, discovered in the area of the Holy Sepulchre Church, attests that this area was then beyond the city walls. The view has recently been advanced that both the Hill of Golgotha and the area of the Church of the Holy Sepulchre served as burial areas similar to the burial area in the Kidron Valley.

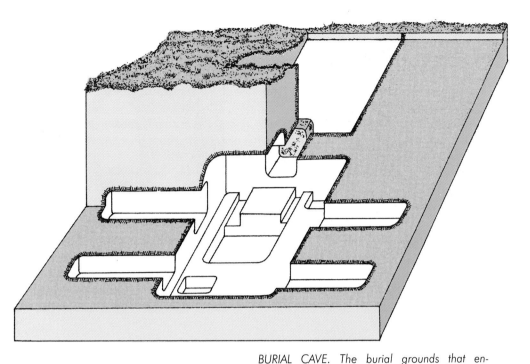

BURIAL CAVE. The burial grounds that encompassed Jerusalem in the Second Temple period extended from what is known today as French Hill in the north to Ramat Rahel in the south, and from Mount Scopus in the east to Beit Hakerem in the west. Shown here is the plan of a typical family burial cave of that time in the city's graveyards. Entry to the cave was through a small opening off a courtyard hewn out of the rock. In the entrance hall was a pit into which the bones of the deceased had been cast. The ossuaries containing the remains were placed in niches (kokhs) hewn out of the rock for this purpose.

JEWISH COIN (obverse) from the time of the Great Revolt (69 BCE.), that shows a motif of three pomegranates joined together. The inscription "Jerusalem the Holy" is significant in that the attempt to preserve the Jewish nature of Jerusalem was one of the causes of the revolt.

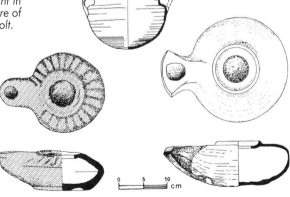

OFFERINGS FOR THE DEAD. The pottery vessels shown are examples of donations found in graves, placed there as offerings for the dead. Glass vessels and coins were also sometimes placed in the graves.

25

The Third Wall was begun by King Agrippa (ca. 44 CE). For various reasons he was unable to complete the project — a task left to a later generation who fortified it during the War against the Romans (66-70 CE). The Beth Zetha (or Bezetha) district added to the city limits by this wall was nearly uninhabited at the time of the construction of the Third Wall; but it greatly enhanced the total area of Jerusalem. (The area within the walls at that time measured about four square kilometres — as against less than one square kilometre today). Josephus Flavius relates that the towers built along the wall bore the name 'Women's Towers' for no apparent reason.

So far, remains have been discovered of the northern segment of this wall only, mainly in the excavations carried out by the late Professors Sukenik and Mayer. No traces have been found, on the other hand, of those sections that connected the northern wall with the other walls to the south, with one possible exception: remains of an ancient structure discovered underneath a tower to the east of the Church of St. Anne in the Old City. This may indicate that the eastern section of the Third Wall may have passed here. In addition to sturdy walls, the fortifications of Jerusalem included fortresses. From ancient times, an imposing fortress called The Stronghold ('Ha-Bira') had stood at the northwestern edge of the Temple Mount, on an elevation that was slightly higher than the Temple itself. It appears that Herod demolished this fortress and, in its place, erected the Antonia Fortress. The rock on which this fort was built was hewn on all sides, thus creating a steep hill crowned by the fortress. A large cistern known as the Struthion Pool was cut into the rock at the base of the citadel, drawing water from the drainage basin of the adjacent Tyropoeon Valley. Our sources relate that this fortress had four towers, one of which was named Straton. While nothing is left of the fort itself, the hewn surface of the rock on which it stood enables us to arrive at a rough estimate of its dimensions: 100 metres long, 35 metres wide. The fortress served to protect the Temple Mount. Its fall during the war against Rome paved the way for the conquest of the Temple Mount and the fall of Jerusalem.

A second fortress was built by Herod in another strategic spot on the city's circumference — the northwestern corner of the Upper City, where the terrain forms a 'saddle' between the Citadel Valley (leading into the Hinnom Valley) and the Transversal Valley (which runs down into the Tyropoeon Valley). This fortress was formed by three towers — Hippicus, Mariamme and Phasael. For this reason, it is called the Towers' Fortress, and the water reservoir just to the north of it — the Towers' Pool. All that remains of this fortress today is the base of one of its towers, apparently the Hippicus Tower, from which the Third Wall proceeded northward. It is on this base and its later superstructure which is popularly known today as 'David's Tower.'

During the Hasmonean era, and especially in the days of King Herod, many magnificent buildings were erected in Jerusalem — first and foremost among them, of course, the Temple. There were also a theatre, surmised to have been located in the Upper City, and a marketplace — this too in the Upper City. No trace remains of either. All that is left today of Herod's magnificent walled palace in the Upper City, is part of the substructured filling upon which the grand edifice had been erected. The remains of the palace itself vanished in the days of the Crusaders, who replaced it with a new royal palace for the Crusader monarchs. The historian Josephus Flavius reports on another project executed at that time: a monument at the tomb of King David which, according to an already contemporary tradition, was located on Mount Zion. According to the New Testament, the Upper City also was the site of the mansions of the High Priests. Josephus mentions other buildings erected in the Upper City - such as the Hasmonean Palace, the Council Building and others. Again, no vestiges remain of any of these structures, so that it is impossible for us today to identify their precise location.

What does emerge, however, from the excavations conducted in the Upper City is that this was a well-planned city. Its dwellings were those of the well-to-do, some of them indeed impressive multistoried structures, adorned with wall paintings and mosaic floors.

THE ROYAL TOMBS. Under the influence of eastern Hellenistic architecture, and of the biblical prohibition against fashioning graven images, a characteristic Jewish architectural style developed in Jerusalem that found its particular expression in the first century BCE and the first century CE up to the destruction of the Second Temple (70 CE). This style is manifested especially in the elaborate facades of tombs found in the vicinity of the city and dating to this period. A fine example of the art is shown in the above sketch, showing the facade of the tombs of Queen Helena and her family. The facade was topped by three pyramids, and the entire structure stood at the end of a spacious courtyard hewn from the rock, into which one descended by a set of stairs. Embossed on the cornice were a variety of fruits and plants such as grape clusters, flower wreaths, acanthus leaves and others — all in the Hellenistic style typical of the period.

SARCOPHAGUS. This stone coffin from Herod's Family Tombs bears a typically Jewish decoration.

JERUSALEM AT
THE TIME OF JESUS

In the time of Jesus, the city generally appeared as is shown on the map of Jerusalem at the end of the Second Temple period. The Third Wall, however, and the suburb of Bezetha included within it, were built some years after his death.

The city which Jesus knew was the Herodian Jerusalem, with its rebuilt Temple Compound. The rebuilding of the Temple and its beautiful appearance are mentioned in the Gospels.

The New Testament is sparing in descriptions of Jerusalem, and generally goes into detail only when the narrative requires it. Usually, it mentions only the name of a place without any distinguishing feature which would help us to identify it today. Moreover, matters are further complicated by the fact that during their periods of domination in the city, Christians built churches and other commemorative buildings on sites of doubtful authenticity which nevertheless, in the course of time, have gained the sanction of tradition. If we attempt to reconstruct the appearance of the city in the time of Jesus, we must disregard these buildings and the traditions surrounding them, and confine ourselves to the historical sources and archaeological finds. If we do so, the number of holy sites will be drastically reduced, but we will gain a clearer picture of them. Our reconstruction will draw on certain sources: 1) Extra-canonical literary works of the period, such as the writings of Josephus Flavius; with his help we can locate, for example, Solomon's Porch, mentioned in John 10:23 and Acts 3:11 etc. 2) Archaeological excavations, which have yielded evidence concerning, for instance, the pinnacle of the Temple (Matthew 4:5, Luke 4:9), or the Antonia Fortress containing the Praetorium, mentioned several times in the Gospels (there is a fairly accurate description in John 19:5-13).

Nowadays it seems doubtful whether Pontius Pilate actually resided in the Antonia Fortress. Some scholars suggest he may have resided at the Hasmonean Palace located over the eastern cliff of the present Jewish Quarter. But others presume he would have preferred the luxurious palace of Herod, south of the present Citadel. Acceptance of any one of these theories would necessitate a change in the course of the Via Dolorosa. But in this map, we have attempted a scientific, though hypothetical, reconstruction of the Way of the Cross. The route which was arrived at is not so very different from the one shown today to tourists, which is curious enough in view of the fact that the tradition on which it is based is very late. Generally, we have avoided including in the map places not mentioned in the New Testament or sanctified only by later periods. An exception is the Judgement Gate, today within the Russian Hospice; remains of a gate, which could well date from the time of Jesus, have been found on this site giving easy access to the Holy Sepulchre.

Judging from archaeological evidence alone, nothing contradicts the siting of the Holy Sepulchre at the actual site where it is believed to be today. Corroborating this view is the fact that a few Jewish tombs have been found enclosed within the nearby rotunda. Among them are those traditionally ascribed to Nicodemus and Joseph of Arimathaea, in whose field Jesus was buried.

We have omitted the Stations of the Cross, because they are merely traditional and lack scientific authentication. This is also true of some other sites, such as the Crusader (or

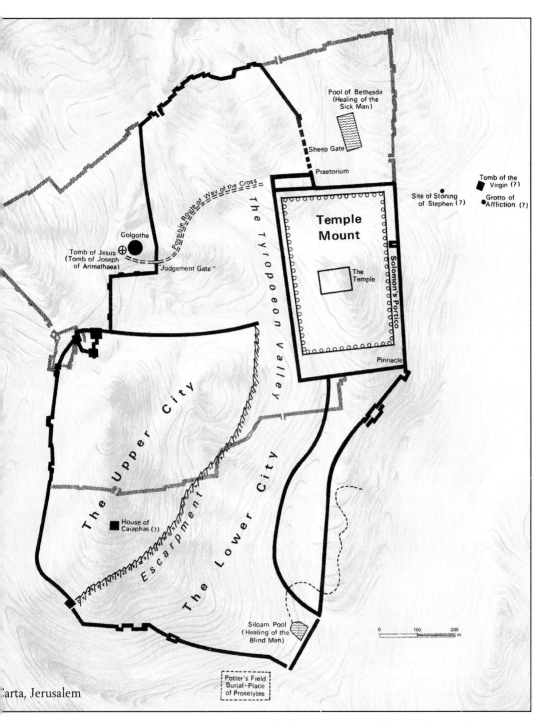

Pool of Bethesda
(Healing of the
Sick Man)

Sheep Gate

Praetorium

Site of Stoning
of Stephen (?)

Tomb of the
Virgin (?)

Grotto of
Affliction (?)

Possible Route of Way of the Cross

The Tyropoeon valley

Golgotha

Temple
Mount

Tomb of Jesus
(Tomb of Joseph
of Arimathaea)

"Judgement Gate"

The Temple

Solomon's Portico

Pinnacle

The Upper City

The Lower City

House of
Caiaphas (?)

Escarpment

Siloam Pool
(Healing of the
Blind Man)

0   100   200
m

Carta, Jerusalem

Potter's Field
Burial-Place
of Proselytes

perhaps even Byzantine) remains on Mt. Zion, including the Coenaculum. With regard to many sites, various churches have conflicting traditions as to where an event took place, which only serves to add to the confusion. The Catholics and Armenians, for example, each claim their own site for the House of Caiaphas, and similar disagreements exist in many other cases.

THE ROMAN PERIOD
70-330 CE

Insofar as it must rely on written sources, our knowledge of this period in the history of Jerusalem is extremely scanty. Jewish sources are few, and Christian sources are mostly from the Byzantine period and in the main are concerned with describing the difficulties that faced Christian pilgrims wishing to visit their holy places in Jerusalem. In recent times, however, there has been a steady increase in the archaeological finds connected with the Roman period.

In his *The Jewish War* (7,1,1), the contemporary historian Josephus Flavius relates that, following the Jewish revolt against Rome which ended in the destruction of the Temple and the capture of Jerusalem in the year 70 CE, the Emperor Titus decided "to demolish the entire city... and to leave intact (only) the three towers — Phasael, Hippicus and Mariamme — and that portion of the wall bounding the city on the west, in order to provide a place for the Roman garrison that was to remain in Jerusalem, and in order that these towers might stand as mute testimony, for later generations, to the epic story of the great city with its strong, fortified defences, overcome by the might and bravery of Rome."

In point of fact, excavations carried out at the site of the Citadel and along the city's western wall reveal that the vestiges of Second Temple Jerusalem found here were to remain intact throughout the Roman period.

A number of finds give evidence of the presence of the garrison force — Rome's Tenth Legion — which set up camp in the area of what is today the Armenian Garden. Near a structure in the Citadel, for example, a water pipe was found bearing the Legion's seal. In the Armenian Garden itself, numerous small objects were found (such as Tenth Legion seals) attesting to the Legion's presence in the area. Many pieces of roof-tiles, moreover, believed to have belonged to the Tenth Legion, provide further evidence of Roman settlement in the area. The tiles were manufactured in Jerusalem, where, to date, two major supply centres have been found — one of them in the area of today's Convention Centre (Binyenei Ha'oomah), and the other in the vicinity of Ramat Rahel, on Jerusalem's southern outskirts. The Tenth Legion represented a substantial proportion of the city's population in the Roman period; Titus, moreover, brought some 800 retired Roman soldiers to help repopulate Jerusalem.

No information is available on the fate and condition of the Jews who remained in Jerusalem after the war. Epiphanius observes that on Mount Zion there remained seven synagogues after the destruction of the Temple, one of these surviving until the reign of Emperor Constantine in the fourth century. If the reference is not to Christian houses of worship, the above observation is proof that a Jewish community did exist in Jerusalem at this time.

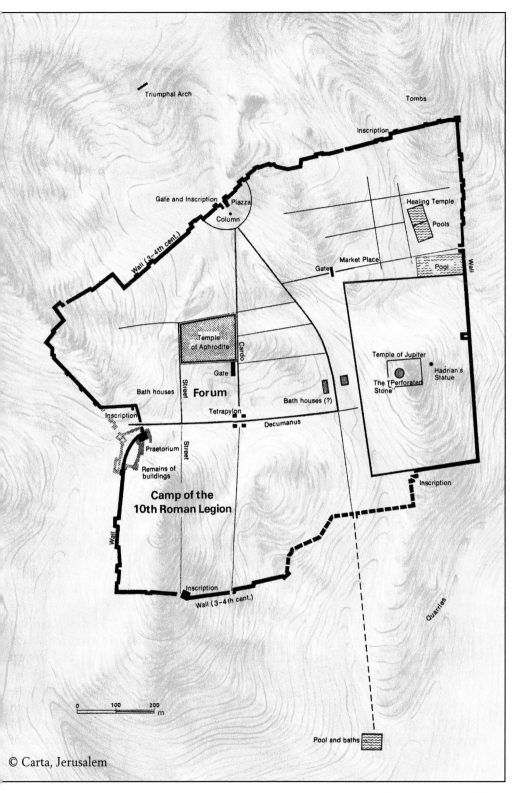

Triumphal Arch

Tombs

Inscription

Gate and Inscription · Piazza
· Column

Healing Temple

Pools

Wall (3–4th cent.)

Market Place

Gate

Pool

Wall

Temple
of Aphrodite

Cardo

Temple of Jupiter

Hadrian's
Statue

The "Perforated
Stone"

Gate

Forum

Bath houses

Street

Bath houses (?)

Inscription

Tetrapylon

Decumanus

Street

Praetorium

Remains of
buildings

Inscription

Camp of the
10th Roman Legion

Wall

Inscription

Wall (3–4th cent.)

Quarries

0   100   200
                m

Pool and baths

© Carta, Jerusalem

0 1 2 m

Section of the Ecce Homo Arch
in the Sisters of Zion Convent.

Central archway of
Ecce Homo Arch.

In the year 132 the Bar-Kokhba revolt erupted. One of the reasons for the revolt was the establishment of the Roman city Aelia Capitolina in place of Jerusalem. The decision concerning the establishment of the Roman city was taken by Emperor Hadrian, following his visit to the East in 129. The name was composed of two elements: Aelia — after the Emperor himself, whose full name was Publius Aelius Hadrianus; and Capitolina — after the deities appointed to be the patrons of the new city, the Capitolina triad: Jupiter, Juno and Minerva. The worship of these deities was later to be instituted in the temple erected in their honour on the Temple Mount. The city also was to have the usual municipal institutions, mentioned in a fifth century Christian source: "...two public baths, a theatre, the Tricameron, the Tetranympheum, the Dodecapylon and the Temple Mount, and he divided the city into seven wards, appointing a warden for each..." Clearly, the reference here is to repairs made to the Temple Mount enclosure. The Tricameron would appear to be the sanctuary erected for the three patron-deities. The Tetranympheum was a pool with four rows of pillars, next to the Siloam Pool.

All that remains of the Roman temple erected on the Temple Mount is a dedication to

THE ECCE HOMO ARCH. Theories have varied, through the ages, as to the actual route of the Via Dolorosa. In all of the theories, however, the arch, erroneously called the Ecce Homo Arch, is listed as one of the Stations of the Cross. This is the spot, it was commonly believed, where the Roman Governor, Pontius Pilate, brought Jesus before the people and said, "Behold the man!" (Ecce Homo). When the Convent of the Sisters of Zion was built in 1864, part of the arch was incorporated into the new building. Archaeological explorations within the convent's church, however, revealed that the arch is not from the Second Temple period at all, but is one of a series of triumphal arches erected by Emperor Hadrian about a century later. There is also a recent hypothesis that the area had been a market and that this arch stood at its western entrance. In any event, it is now quite certain that the arch was in no way connected with Pontius Pilate's residence, the Antonio Fortress.

MEMORIAL TABLET. The inscription commemorates the Tenth Legion Commander, Marcus Junius. Found near the Jaffa Gate.

Emperor Hadrian Inscribed on one of the building stones above the Double Gate. The inscription reads: "To Titus Aelius Hadrianus, Antonius Augustus the Pious, Father of the Homeland, the Prophet-Priest — Placed at the behest of the ten Heads of the City." It would appear that several of the 'patches' visible to this day in the revetment walls of the Temple Mount Compound may be attributed to the Roman period.

In the excavations carried out in the courtyard of St. Anne's Church, near today's Lions' (or St. Stephen's) Gate, two tremendous pools were uncovered. In ancient times, it was believed that the waters in these pools had special healing qualities, and in the Roman period a temple was erected there to the Roman god of healing, Asclepius, as evidenced by the sculpted snake, symbol of this deity, which was found here. Those seeking the cure apparently spent the night in partly subterranean cave-like structures serving this purpose, and immersed themselves in small pools installed adjacent to the large ones. The place must have been rather popular with the inhabitants of Jerusalem, judging from the numerous sculptures and figurines found in the area, apparently left there by grateful customers as gifts to the temple.

That there was once a commercial centre in the eastern part of the city became known only a few years ago, when the base of the Ecce Homo Arch was examined. (According to Christian tradition, the arch is one of the Stations on the Via Dolorosa, where the Roman Consul Pontius Pilate pointed to Jesus and said: "Behold the man!"). It was concluded that this arch served as a kind of entrance-way to a large marketplace, extensive portions of whose paved square are now sheltered by the adjacent Convent of the Sisters of Zion. The buildings belonging to this market were arranged around the square, some of them hewn in the rock. Underneath the market square there is a large pool — the Struthion Pool — dating from the Second Temple period when it served as a source of water for the market. The arch itself is the top portion of the central part of a wide entrance-gate composed of three arched entrances — a large one in the centre, flanked by two smaller ones. This style of gateway was a common feature of Roman architecture, especially in the second century. At least three more such gateways were found in various parts of Jerusalem. One of these, probably the most imposing of the three, spanned the road leading out of Jerusalem northward — about 400 metres to the north of the Damascus Gate. The top-

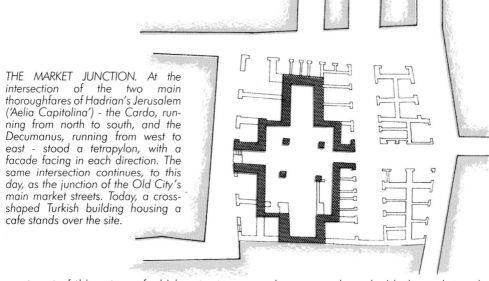

THE MARKET JUNCTION. At the intersection of the two main thoroughfares of Hadrian's Jerusalem ('Aelia Capitolina') - the Cardo, running from north to south, and the Decumanus, running from west to east - stood a tetrapylon, with a facade facing in each direction. The same intersection continues, to this day, as the junction of the Old City's main market streets. Today, a cross-shaped Turkish building housing a cafe stands over the site.

most part of this gate — of which not a trace remains — was adorned with the sculptured likeness of Hadrian and a dedicatory inscription.

Another gate in the same style stood at the northeastern entry to the City Forum, which was located in the area of the present-day Muristan. The remains of this gate are to be found today in the Russian Church. Little has remained of the Forum itself: a few walls at the southern end of the Church of the Holy Sepulchre; sections of the paved marketplace, discovered in excavations underneath the Lutheran Church of the Redeemer; and water collection and drainage systems serving the market discovered during the excavations of Kathleen Kenyon.

The vestiges of yet another gate, again in the same style, are to be found to this day under the Damascus Gate. It appears that for many years this gateway stood by itself, outside the city wall, serving as a kind of welcoming arch for visitors to the city. The fact that it was made of Herodian-style hewn stones is not necessarily evidence that it was built in Herod's time; it could have been constructed with stones taken from the ruins of buildings destroyed in the Romans' war against the Jews in 66-70 CE. An inscription added to the gateway reads: "To the Colony of Aelia Capitolina — at the behest of the Heads of the City."

According to Christian sources, the spot on which the Church of the Holy Sepulchre stands was once occupied by a temple to the Roman goddess Aphrodite, erected by Hadrian. Further evidence that this spot once held a prominent Roman public building is provided by the findings of the archaeological research that has been carried out for many years now at and around the site of the Holy Sepulchre Church. The most prominent vestige of that temple is the entablature (the frieze and cornice that rested on the columns of the building) that now serves as a cornice on the facade of the Holy Sepulchre Church. Other traces of the Roman temple were discovered east of the Chapel of Helena, within the Holy Sepulchre Church, and they include the drawing of a ship, with an inscription beneath it — the work of a Christian pilgrim, perhaps in payment of a pledge.

Some information about the Jerusalem of Roman times is provided by the inscriptions on Roman tombstones. While the site of the cemetery itself has not been located, a number of its tombstones, used in the Byzantine period already as building stones, have been found in various sections of the city. The inscriptions generally provide personal information about the lives of the deceased, and from some of them we learn of the adventures of Roman soldiers prior to their being stationed in Jerusalem.

It is difficult to say just when Jerusalem took on the shape indicated in our map. Examination of the northern wall in various places has revealed that this wall was built at the end of the third or the beginning of the fourth century — about the time when the Romans are known to have put up similar walls in other towns of the country. It would appear that so long as the Tenth Legion was ensconced inside the city, its presence sufficed to give Jerusalem the physical security it needed. When, however, at the end of the third century, the Legion was moved to Eilat, as part of the reorganization of the boundaries of the Roman Empire, it became necessary to base the city's military defences on a system of fortifications, the main feature of which was the city wall. On Jerusalem's eastern and western sides, use was made of the vestiges of the Second Temple period walls; in the north and the south, on the other hand, entirely new walls were erected. The nearly square shape of Jerusalem which was developed in this period, and which served to facilitate the defence of the city, remained intact until the middle of the 19th century, when Jerusalem began to spread beyond its walls.

The pattern of the city's streets has its origins in the pattern of Roman army camps, which featured a rectangular arrangement of streets running the length and breadth of the camp and intersecting at right angles. Two main streets — the western Cardo and the eastern Cardo — connected the gate in the northern wall (today the Damascus Gate) with the two gates in the southern wall (Zion and Dung Gates). The lateral street — the Decumanus — ran from the western gate (Jaffa Gate) to the eastern gate (today the Gate of the Chain). This route continued through the eastern Cardo northwards and resumed its course eastwards to the Lions' Gate of today. However, the area between the western Cardo and the eastern Cardo, in the southern part of the city, was not yet populated in the Roman era; and while it may be said that the general shape of the city was determined in this period, Jerusalem did not receive its final form until the Byzantine era (viz. *Israel Exploration Journal*, Vol.27,p.56).

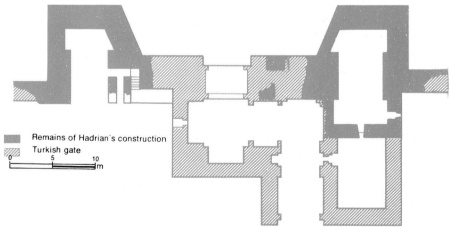

Remains of Hadrian's construction
Turkish gate
0   5   10
m

DAMASCUS GATE. Built by the Sultan Suleiman the Magnificent, it stands partly on the site of a Roman gate that appears to have been built when the city was fortified in the third century. The Roman gate was a freestanding structure (not connected with the wall) and was possibly a triumphal arch erected in 136 CE, when 'Aelia Capitolina' was founded. As was the custom in those days, the large central arch was flanked by two smaller ones. The Roman gate may have been constructed of stones taken from the ruins of an earlier structure nearby. Not far from this spot, the remains have been found of a gate dating from the Herodian period.

THE BYZANTINE PERIOD
330-638 CE

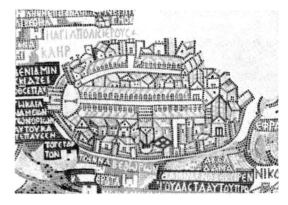

SECTION OF MADABA MAP showing 6th century Jerusalem.

When Christianity became a state religion, Jerusalem became a religious and spiritual centre for the entire Christian world. Jerusalem now came under the control of a new group of masters, with new ambitions and new demands in all that concerned the spiritual role of the city, its status and its physical shape. This period, then, is distinguished by a great upsurge of building activity — with the accent on the monumental and the magnificent.

One of the sources of our knowledge concerning Jerusalem in the Byzantine era is the pilgrims' literature, which steadily grew in volume during this period. Another important source is the Madaba Map— a sixth-century mosaic map, discovered in a church in the town of Madaba, east of the Jordan River. The map depicts the land of Israel, its towns and cities. Jerusalem is presented on this map on a scale of approximately 1:1600, and the portrayal of the city furnishes us with many details concerning its shape and its components. Yet another major source of information is to be found in the descriptions of Thomas the Undertaker: Thomas engaged in the burial of victims of the Persian slaughter at the time of the Persian conquest of Jerusalem in 614, and he describes the places he encountered in the course of this activity.

One thing revealed by these sources is that the general outlines of the city as they existed at the end of the Roman period continued for quite a long time into the Byzantine period as well. There came a time, however, when Jerusalem again expanded, northward and southward, beyond the Roman walls. In the fifth century a large monastery was erected to the north of the city — St. Stephen's Church (on the Nablus Road, on the spot where today the Church of St; Etienne stands).

Settlement beyond the northern wall in Byzantine times is likewise attested to by the remains of various buildings dating from that period, some containing beautiful mosaic floors, dug up in the 19th century as well as in more recent archaeological excavations.

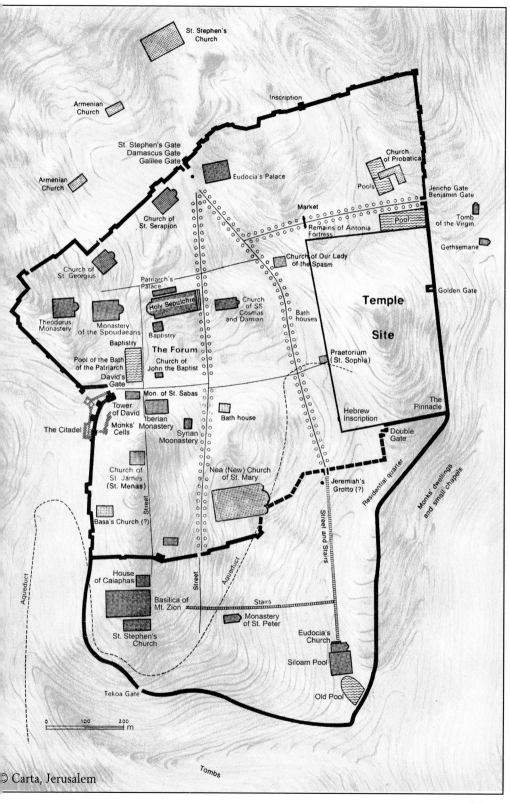

St. Stephen's Church

Armenian Church

Inscription

St. Stephen's Gate
Damascus Gate
Galilee Gate

Armenian Church

Eudocia's Palace

Church of Probatica

Pools

Church of St. Serapion

Market

Remains of Antonia Fortress

Jericho Gate
Benjamin Gate

Pool

Tomb of the Virgin

Church of Our Lady of the Spasm

Gethsemane

Church of St. Georgius

Patriarch's Palace

Golden Gate

Theodorus Monastery

Monastery of the Spoudaeans

Holy Sepulchre

Church of SS Cosmas and Damian

Bath houses

Temple Site

Baptistry

The Forum

Baptistry

Church of John the Baptist

Praetorium (St. Sophia)

Pool of the Bath of the Patriarch

David's Gate

Mon. of St. Sabas

Hebrew Inscription

The Pinnacle

Tower of David

The Citadel

Monks' Cells

Iberian Monastery

Bath house

Syrian Monastery

Double Gate

Church of St. James (St. Menas)

Nea (New) Church of St. Mary

Jeremiah's Grotto (?)

Residential quarter

Monks' dwellings and small chapels

Basa's Church (?)

Street

Street and Stairs

Aqueduct

House of Caiaphas

Street

Aqueduct

Stairs

Basilica of Mt. Zion

Monastery of St. Peter

Eudocia's Church

St. Stephen's Church

Siloam Pool

Aqueduct

Tekoa Gate

Old Pool

0   100   200
m

Tombs

© Carta, Jerusalem

THE DOUBLE GATE. A 7th century (?) Byzantine addition to the Second Temple Hulda Gate.

With the population of Jerusalem spreading southward, too, beyond the old Roman walls, a number of churches were built in this area, and it became necessary to put up a new wall further south. This was done in the fifth century, after the Empress Eudocia came to Jerusalem. The new wall — like that of the Second Temple era, on whose foundations it was built — encompassed the City of David as well as Mount Zion. The only gate to be added to the wall during the Byzantine period was the Gate of Mercy (also known as 'the Golden Gate') in the eastern segment, built apparently during the reign of Emperor Heraclius to celebrate the return of the Cross to the Holy City (629) — after it fell to the Persians (614).

The pattern of the city's streets remained basically the same as it had been in Roman times. The square facing Damascus Gate, with a column standing in its centre, is clearly discernible in the Madaba Map. The column may have been a holdover from the Roman period, as was the case with other columns found elsewhere — such as the Trajan and

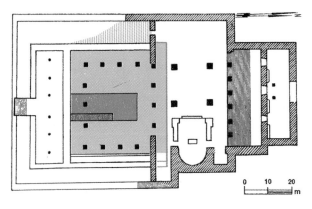

THE SILOAM POOL. This pool, which is as old as Jerusalem itself, is traditionally held sacred by the Christians because it was here that the blind man was healed by Jesus' instruction. To commemorate this event the Empress Eudocia built a church beyond the pool in the 5th century. From the pool, which was enlarged and surrounded by a shady colonnade, a flight of steps led northwards to the basilica-shaped church, and beyond the church another flight of stairs led upwards to the city. The present pool (4 by 16 metres) has been dug out in part from the earlier pool.

0   10   20
|___|___| m

Aurelius Columns in Rome. These columns were generally topped off with the bust of a Roman Emperor – in Jerusalem this being, presumably, that of the Emperor Hadrian. The Jerusalem column is commemorated to this day in the Arabic name of the gate nearby – Bab el-Ammud (Gate of the Column); in Hebrew, it is known as Sha'ar Shechem (Nablus Gate) and in English as Damascus Gate.

From the square at Damascus Gate, two arterial roads radiated in a generally southward direction: one (the western Cardo) led to the Zion Gate, the other (the eastern Cardo) to the Dung Gate. Both of these thoroughfares were flanked by rows of pillars, and the streets themselves were covered. Sections of a third major road, running parallel to the western Cardo and to the west of it, have been discovered in recent years; it is presumed that this road may have run through today's Armenian Quarter to Mount Zion, where traces of it have been uncovered. Altogether, six parallel roads have been discovered, in the City of David and on Mount Zion, running north-to-south; their width follow one of three standard measures: 12, 18 or 72 Byzantine feet (1 Byzantine foot = 30.5 cm).

As in Roman times, the Byzantine city was divided into quarters. The Temple Mount was a quarter in itself. Although the Mount was considered a holy place, there is no evidence of any noteworthy structures having been put up on it in Byzantine times. The Madaba Map shows a gate in the eastern wall that may have preceded the Golden Gate. At the southeastern edge of the Temple Mount, also known as the 'Temple Mount Corner,' the Madaba Map indicates the existence of a structure that is not further identified. According to Christian tradition, this is the place where Jesus was tempted by Satan, and it is possible that a building was erected there to commemorate that event; in any case, some of the pilgrims of this era mention the building at the Temple Mount Corner.

A large area shown rather prominently at the southwestern corner of the Temple Mount is believed by some scholars to represent the Western Wall ('Wailing Wall'), which apparently was considered a major site in this part of the city.

We cannot with certainty identify the structure depicted on the map at the northwestern corner of the Mount; perhaps it represents the remains of the Antonia Fortress.

One of Jerusalem's more important churches, St. Sophia's Church, was built in the Byzantine period on the strip of land between the Temple Mount and the eastern Cardo, on the spot where, according to Christian tradition, Jesus was flagellated and tried in court. The remains of this church appear to be buried beneath the large Crusader structure (a church?) discovered a few years ago during clearing operations in the Western Wall area north of Wilson's Arch. Several of the pilgrims of that era testified that, not far from St. Sophia's Church, they were shown "the pit into which the Prophet Jeremiah had been cast." Recently, the site was identified just beyond the Dung Gate, as workers were widening the road leading from that gate to Mount Zion.

Among the buildings erected in the southeastern quarter of Jerusalem (today's Jewish Quarter), mention must first of all be made of the 'Nea' (New) Church, a large building erected by the Emperor Justinian and dedicated in the year 540. The remains of this church were uncovered in excavations conducted at the southern edge of the Jewish Quarter, in the area of the Almshouses; indeed, some traces of the building were found outside the present city wall. Not much has been preserved of the church itself, but there are some very impressive remains of the support-structures. There are also traces of some ancillary structures related to the church (hostels, storehouses, a library, home for the aged, etc.). From this church eastward to today's Dung Gate and beyond, stretched a residential area that has so far proved to be the most densely settled area of that period in the Old City.

INSCRIPTION OF THE 'NEA' CHURCH. This inscription, found on one of the walls of the support-structure in the 'Nea' Church, reads: "And this is the work which our most pious Emperor Flavius Justinianus carried out with munificence, under the care and devotion of the most holy Constantinus, Priest and Hegumen in the 13th year of the indiction." The inscription proves not only that this building was built by the Emperor Justinian in the year 540, but also that this church was, in fact, the 'Nea' Church.

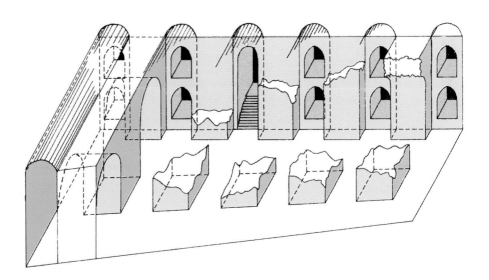

THE NEW CHURCH OF THE VIRGIN MARY ('NEA'). Built by Justinian, it was the most beautiful church in Jerusalem during the Byzantine period. After several years of searching, remains of this church were discovered in the Jewish Quarter. Although parts still remain uncovered, it is possible to imagine from what has been revealed the proportions of the building.

Most impressive are the support-structures built for the church (due to the difficult terrain on which it was built). These support-structures, portrayed in the above plan, were already discerned in the last century, although only recently have they been revealed in their entirety. The supports were also utilized as water cisterns for the church.

A few churches were built outside the southern wall of the Roman city during the Byzantine era, in areas which were later encompassed by a new wall. At the bottom of the Tyropoeon Valley stood the Siloam Church, erected by the Empress Eudocia in the middle of the fifth century. This church, excavated in the years 1894-97, was built around the Siloam Pool. Since its excavation, it has been completely destroyed. Nearby was St. Peter's Church, where pilgrims were shown the house of Caiaphas — the High Priest in Jesus' time. Also exhibited here was the pillar to which, according to Christian tradition, Jesus was tied on the occasion of his flagellation. This pillar was later transferred to the Basilica of Mount Zion, regarded as the mother church of Jerusalem. It was erected on the spot where several events connected with Jesus are said to have transpired: here Jesus washed the feet of his disciples; here his mother Mary died; and here the Holy Ghost descended upon the disciples of Jesus before Jesus revealed himself on the Feast of the Pentecost. The Basilica of Mount Zion, which also exhibited the Crown of Thorns placed on Jesus' head, was highly esteemed among the Christian pilgrims who came to Jerusalem, and it is perhaps the oldest Christian holy place in Jerusalem. Next to this church, a building was erected in the memory of St. Stephen —first of the Christian martyrs, according to tradition. It was in this building that Stephen's body was interred, until it was transferred, at the behest of the Empress Eudocia, to St. Stephen's Church, in the northern part of the city, where today St. Etienne's Church stands.

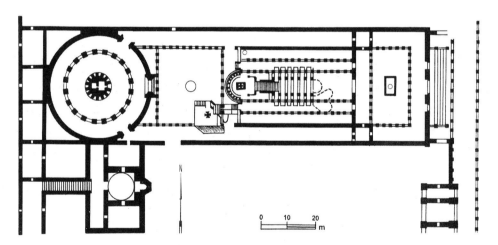

THE CHURCH OF THE HOLY SEPULCHRE. Since Byzantine times this church has been considered the most significant Christian building in the city. Erected by the Emperor Constantine, when his mother Helena discovered the site of the Holy Cross, this church was consecrated in 335 CE. It was built on the site of Hadrian's temple to Aphrodite. On the eastern side of the church, three doorways led into an open colonnaded courtyard which faced the main body of the church, the Martyrium, along whose length stand four rows of pillars which form five prayer aisles. Its size was 26 by 45 metres. The direction of prayer was westwards — an unusual feature of church architecture. From the Martyrium 's centre, a flight of steps descended to a chapel named after Helena, and then continued further down to the spot where she found the True Cross. West of the church is a large colonnaded courtyard, at whose south-eastern corner was the site of the Crucifixion (Golgotha). To the west of the garden was a golden-domed round structure (called the Rotunda or Anastasis) which contained the Holy Sepulchre itself. The Byzantine church was destroyed in 614 CE leaving very few remains of its original structure. The church, as it exists today, dates mainly from the Crusader period.

A CHRISTIAN PILGRIM'S DRAWING AND INSCRIPTION. In excavations conducted in the lower portions of the Church of the Holy Sepulchre, vestiges of a prior structure on this spot - the Temple of Aphrodite - were found. In one of the corners of this structure, a stone was discovered and on it the likeness of a vessel with the inscription underneath it: DOMINE IVIMUS, meaning 'Let us go to the Lord.' From the fact that the inscription is in Latin (rather than in Greek) we may deduce that it was written by a Christian pilgrim who had come to Jerusalem from the western part of the Empire. Conceivably, the writer may have acted clandestinely, so as not to incur the wrath of the priests of the goddess whose temple stood on this hallowed ground (early fourth century). The drawing of the ship is an allusion, apparently, to the route followed by the pilgrim as he made his way to the Holy Land.

The northeastern quarter of Jerusalem had its own attractions for the Christian pilgrim in the Byzantine era. Among these were the Pools of Bethesda, or Sheep's Pools. These pools — and perhaps also the Pool of Israel — were linked to the miracle of the healing of the paralysed man which Christian tradition ascribes to Jesus. To commemorate the miracle, a church in the style of a basilica was erected on the thick wall that separated the two Sheep's Pools. Nearby the place was pointed out where tradition has it that Mary, the Mother of Jesus, was born; and this may be the spot where the Crusaders were, in a later century, to build St. Anne's Church.

As in earlier periods, the hub of political power continued to centre on the Citadel. The main quarter of the city, where most of the public institutions and buildings were located, was the Northwestern Quarter. Undoubtedly the most important of these buildings was the Church of the Holy Sepulchre, linked with Jesus' last days on earth. The church was constructed at the start of the fourth century, by the Emperor Constantine, and was composed of four parts: the rotunda, in the centre of which is the Holy Sepulchre, where Jesus was buried; the Holy Garden — at the time an open courtyard in one corner of which was the Golgotha, the place of Jesus' Crucifixion; the Place of the Testimony (Martyrion) — the church itself, built basilica-style; and the forecourt of the church with the gateway leading directly onto the western Cardo. Judging from descriptions of Byzantine pilgrims, it was a magnificent structure, much of it faced with marble and even gold.

Near the Church of the Holy Sepulchre stood the Patriarch's Palace, probably on the spot where today the Greek Patriarchate stands. In his honour the Towers' Pool of Second Temple times was now renamed Tool of the Bath of the Patriarch.' The Roman Forum, in the Muristan of today, continued in use in the Byzantine period; but all that remains of this central square in the heart of Roman and Byzantine Jerusalem are a few water cisterns, some sections of pavement and the vestiges of the northern gateway, to be found today in the domain of the Russian Church. In the southwestern corner of the Forum, in the year 450, the Church of John the Baptist was erected, which stands to this day. From the Madaba Map and from pilgrims' reports, we know of the existence at that time of other churches and monasteries in this quarter that were destroyed or fell into ruin in the course of time, and whose precise locations have not been determined. Turning now to the southwestern quarter of the city (today's Armenian Quarter), we find that already in Byzantine times the quarter contained the Church of St. James, the Armenians' Cathedral; a small church named after Basa; and the Iberian Monastery, known to us mainly through an inscription describing its location as being near 'the Tower of David' (the name that has adhered to this tower from Byzantine times to this day).

Most of the structures of the Byzantine period that are described in this chapter were either destroyed entirely or badly damaged in the Persian invasion under Chosroes II, in the year 614. (An invasion, incidentally, in which local Jewish forces teamed up with the Persians). Many of the demolished structures were rebuilt after the Byzantine army had reconquered the land in 629 — thanks, in large part, to the efforts of the Patriarch Modestos, who sought to restore to Jerusalem its former Christian character. A few years later, however, Jerusalem was conquered by the Moslems — and with this conquest a new chapter was opened in the annals of the city.

וַתֲּהָי וּשׁישׂ לְבֵבְכֶם
וְעַצְמוֹתְיכֶם כַּדֶּשֶׁא

INSCRIPTION. Part of a prophecy from Isaiah (60:14) engraved on the Western Wall of the Temple Mount. It appears that this verse was engraved at a time of stress for the Jewish inhabitants of the city and perhaps owing to some threat on the inscriber, he abandoned his task before he had finished.

THE FIRST MOSLEM PERIOD
638 -1099

The conquest of Jerusalem by the forces of Omar Ibn Khattab in the year 638 marked the beginning of a 450-year period of Moslem rule that ended with the First Crusade at the end of the eleventh century. Little is known, from primary sources, about the Jerusalem of this period. Contemporary Moslem writers who chose Jerusalem as their subject were few, though two of them are worthy of mention: El-Maqdisi, a Jerusalemite who lived at the end of the tenth century, and Nasir-i-Khusrau, a Persian who visited the city in 1047. Christian pilgrims, who continued in this period, too, to visit Jerusalem, are another source of information with their descriptions of places seen on their pilgrimages. Most of our knowledge of Jerusalem in the Arab era, however, must be drawn from later descriptions — specifically, from the Crusader period.

Jerusalem is also sacred to the Moslems — ranking third, in this respect, after Mecca and Medina in the Arabian peninsula — and numerous Moslem traditions are linked with it. Nevertheless, the Moslem conquerors of Palestine did not make Jerusalem their political or administrative capital. After its conquest, many of its Christian inhabitants left the city, to be replaced by Moslems of different origins, including Arabs from the Arabian peninsula. Yet there was little change in the overall aspect of the city, and in many respects life in Jerusalem went on much as before.

In the course of time, there were several changes of dynasty among the Moslem rulers of the city, and of the country as a whole, and with these changes of dynasty came changes in the fortunes of the city. Thus the periods of rule by the Caliphs of the Omayyad (660-750) and Abbasid (750-969) dynasties were regarded as flourishing periods. The period of Fatimid rule (969-1071), on the other hand, marked a decline; and the subsequent conquests of the Seljuks and the Mongols led to even greater disorder and chaos, until finally Jerusalem was captured in 1099 by the Crusaders.

Shortly after the capture of Jerusalem by the Moslems, the Caliph Omar paid a visit to the city. A number of traditions are connected with this visit, and one of these concerns

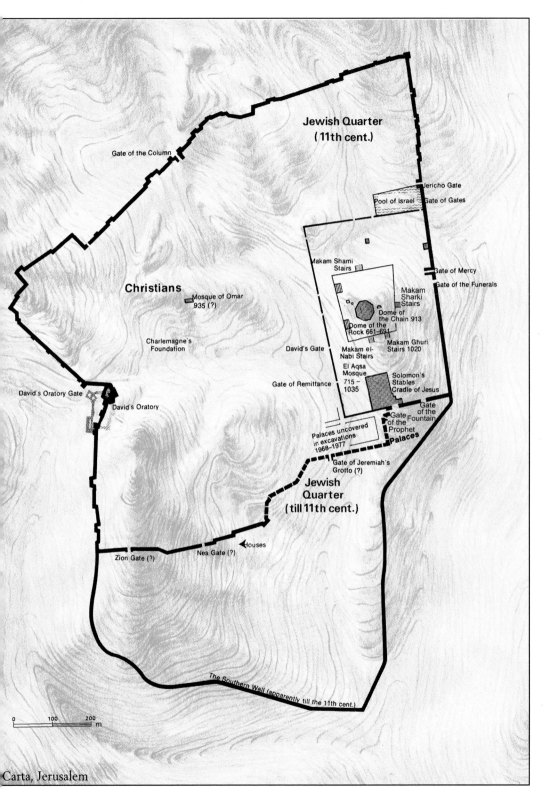

Jewish Quarter
(11th cent.)

Gate of the Column

Jericho Gate

Pool of Israel   Gate of Gates

Makam Shami
Stairs

Gate of Mercy

Christians

Mosque of Omar
935 (?)

Gate of the Funerals

Makam
Sharki
Stairs

Dome of
the Chain 913

Dome of the
Rock 661–691

Charlemagne's
Foundation

David's Gate

Makam Ghuri
Stairs 1020

Makam el-
Nabi Stairs

El Aqsa
Mosque
715 –
1035

Solomon's
Stables
Cradle of Jesus

David's Oratory Gate

Gate of Remittance

David's Oratory

Gate
of the
Fountain

Gate
of the
Prophet

Palaces

Palaces uncovered
in excavations
1968–1977

Gate of Jeremiah's
Grotto (?)

Jewish
Quarter
(till 11th cent.)

Houses

Zion Gate (?)   Nea Gate (?)

The Southern Wall (apparently till the 11th cent.)

0   100   200
                m

Carta, Jerusalem

45

THE EL-AQSA MOSQUE. In the First Moslem period the whole of the Temple Mount was called El-Aqsa, meaning 'the distant place' in Arabic, for this spot was traditionally held to be the destination of Muhammed's Night Journey recorded in the Koran. As a result, the city of Jerusalem and this site in particular became one of the holiest places of Islam. Built over the remains of the Second Temple Hulda Gate, the foundations of the El-Aqsa Mosque are consequently insecure and the building has frequently fallen prey to natural disasters. It was first built in 705 by the Caliph el-Walid al-Malik. In 748 it was destroyed by an earthquake and in 758 it was built anew only to be destroyed a second time by an earthquake in 774. Rebuilt in 820, it was again destroyed in 1033 and then rebuilt in 1035. With the arrival of the Crusaders, the mosque became a church and the headquarters of the Templars, who called it the Temple of Solomon, and held it till Salad in conquered Jerusalem. In 1946 an earthquake again undermined its foundations, and the building has since been continually renovated. In its present form it is a mixture of all the styles that have gone into its making.

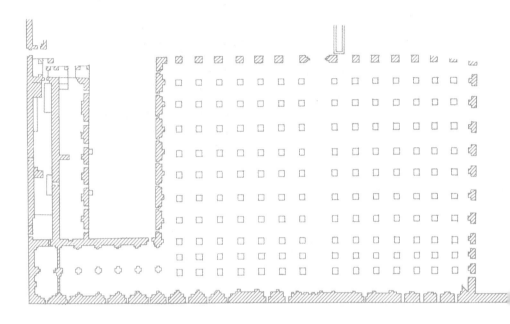

the Temple Mount. It is said that the Caliph was shocked at the stark contrast between the magnificence of the Christian churches in the city and the filth and debris he found on the Temple Mount. Omar ordered the Temple Mount cleaned and a Moslem house of worship to be erected there, on the spot where Israel's Temple had once stood. Indeed, a Christian traveller who visited Jerusalem in the year 670 relates that the Moslems erected on the Temple Mount — on the ruins of what may have been a Roman temple — a square wooden edifice containing places for three thousand worshippers. According to other sources, it appears that the Jews, too, were given certain rights on the Temple Mount, and that it was they who cleaned it.

Another Moslem tradition tells of the construction of the Mosque of Omar next to the Church of the Holy Sepulchre (and not, as is popularly supposed, on the Temple Mount, where the golden-roofed Dome of the Rock is often erroneously referred to as the 'Mosque of Omar'). When Omar arrived in Jerusalem, the Patriarch Sophronius suggested, as a

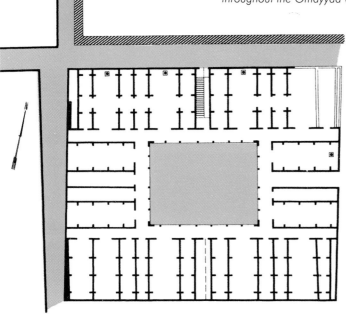

THE OMAYYAD BUILDINGS. The remains of at least four large Early Moslem buildings have been uncovered in Prof. Mazar's excavations around the walls of the Temple Mount since the Six-Day War. These are thought to have been part of the Temple Mount's complex of religious buildings; one has been ascertained as the palace of the Omayyad Caliphs; one possibly served as living-quarters for the religious functionaries; the purpose of the other two is still unclear. The plans of all the buildings are similar: each has a series of rooms divided into separate units, all grouped around a large central chamber. Examples of this plan have been found throughout the Omayyad world, in Iraq, Syria, etc.

mark of honour, that the Caliph worship in the Church of the Holy Sepulchre. Omar declined the offer and, instead, conducted his prayers next to the Church; apparently in commemoration of that event, a mosque was put up just east of the Holy Sepulchre Church.

The Dome of the Rock (really a kind of monument, rather than a mosque) was erected on the Temple Mount in 691, during the reign of the Caliph Abd-el-Malik. This Caliph also saw to the restoration of the city wall and its gates, and he built a government house in the city, although its location has not been found. His son, the Caliph el-Walid, built the El-Aqsa Mosque, at the southern end of the Temple Mount — but here, too, our information concerning its construction is very scant. To this Caliph, too, may be attributed the construction of the monumental palaces uncovered in Prof. Benjamin Mazar's excavations south of the Temple Mount — and also, perhaps, the restoration and embellishment of the Double Gate. The El-Aqsa Mosque, having been constructed on the rough foundations of rubble dating from the Second Temple period, has several times suffered severe damage from earthquakes and on each occasion has had to be restored or

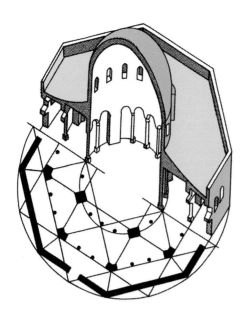

THE DOME OF THE ROCK. An octagonal building on the Temple Mount, 27 metres long and 43 metres high, is the oldest surviving complete example of early Moslem architecture. It was intended not as a place of worship but as a shrine protecting the Foundation Stone - the rock upon which, according to Jewish tradition, Abraham prepared to sacrifice Isaac and which was supposed to have been the site of the Holy of Holies in the First and Second Temples. To Moslems it signified the spot from which Muhammed ascended on his Night Journey. The building was constructed in 691 by Abd-el-Malik and although renovations were made by El-Mamun in the 9th century, and many times since, the building has essentially preserved its original form. Recent renovations during Jordanian rule include the replacement of many of the Turkish tiles on the exterior, and the replacement of the lead dome weighing nearly 200 tons with a dome of aluminium and bronze weighing 35 tons.

rebuilt. The mosque was also damaged during the uprising against the last Caliph of the Omayyad dynasty, which signalled the change-over to rule under the Abbasids. Jerusalem served as a religious focal point for the Abbasid Caliphs, the first few of whom even made pilgrimages to the city (a custom that was to cease later on). Their rule was not, however, marked by any particular achievements in building activity. Two events may be noted in this realm — the renovation of the Dome of the Rock in Caliph Mamun's reign (813-833) and the construction of the Mosque of Omar (935) near the Holy Sepulchre Church.

The decline of Jerusalem in the First Moslem Period began, as has already been indicated, with the conquest of Palestine by the Egyptian Fatimids. In the year 1009, for example, the Caliph El-Haqim (996-1021), in a fit of religious zeal, ordered all the synagogues and churches in the city demolished. There was also a general neglect of the southern city wall during this part of the First Moslem period; it appears that, during the eleventh century, the walls of Jerusalem underwent repairs, except for the southern segment that encompassed the City of David and Mount Zion.

The Holy Sepulchre Church, which fell victim to El-Haqim's order against synagogues and churches in 1009, was restored through the intervention of the Byzantine Emperor in 1047. In 1074, Jerusalem was conquered by the Seljuks, who held it until 1098, when it was captured by the Mongols. A year later, the First Crusade brought the Christians back to Jerusalem.

Since Islam's religious association with Jerusalem was limited largely to the Temple Mount, this was the only part of the city that underwent significant changes during the First Moslem period. From the relatively numerous descriptions of the Temple Mount composed in this period, one is able to glean information about the buildings put up there, and about the various gates and their names. Today we also know the names of the gates in the city wall in that era, and these are shown on the map, in the places where modern historical scholarship places them. The Citadel was then known as 'Mihrab Daoud' (David's Oratory).

Gradually, Jerusalem came to be divided into residential zones according to religious

DOME OF THE ROCK. The most important building of the First Moslem period In Jerusalem, 7th century.

INSCRIPTION. This inscription, found in the Russian Hospice near the Church of the Holy Sepulchre, bears witness to the construction of the Mosque of Omar (935) at the spot where the Caliph offered up his prayers when arriving in Jerusalem.

affiliation. This division was not imposed on the inhabitants of the city, but came about of itself, through the wish of the members of each religious community to live in one area, separate from the members of other faiths. Christians, Moslems and Armenians occupied roughly the same quarters they occupy today. The Jews lived in the quarter near the Dung Gate; towards the end of the period, however, the northern portion of the Moslem Quarter came also to be called the Jewish Quarter.

Jerusalem enjoyed a regular supply of water by means of a system of canals built for this purpose and according to contemporary reports there was no shortage of this vital commodity. The city even contained several bath-houses. A market place, hospices and a church named after the Saviour's mother were first built in the early forum of the city (the Muristan quarter of today), by Europeans during the First Moslem period. The hospices were built for European pilgrims, among them the Hospice of Johanan the Pious, (Patriarch of Alexandria in the seventh century), constructed by merchants from Amalfi. During the Crusader period, the buildings were converted into a hospital named after John the Baptist. The Hospice and the Monastery named after Mary la Latine were built formerly with the aid of Charlemagne. All these structures were included, in Crusader times, in the Hospitallers' Quarter.

From the pilgrims' literature, once again, we learn of the places that Christians visited in this as in the Byzantine period that preceded it: the Church of the Holy Sepulchre, the Tomb of the Virgin and the adjacent Cave of Treachery, the Dome of Ascension on the Mount of Olives, the Basilica of Mount Zion and Gethsemane. (Most of these places are marked on the map of the Byzantine period).

Jewish sources indicate that in this period Jews used to visit places not mentioned previously as Jewish visiting sites, such as the gates of the Temple Mount — the Hulda Gate and the Golden Gate — Absalom's Tomb, and, the focus of visits in that period, a place called 'God's Footstool,' (a large stone found on the heights of the Mount of Olives). Thanks to Moslem descriptions, we know of the synagogues that were in Jerusalem then; their exact locations, however, are not known.

The Moslem writers of the period referred to Jerusalem either as 'Ilya' (a corruption of the Roman and Byzantine 'Aelia') or as 'Bet el-Mukkadas' (Beit Hamikdash, or Temple), apparently inspired by the city's Jews.

THE CRUSADER PERIOD
1099 -1187

The Crusaders ruled in Jerusalem during most of the 12th century. They did in fact again hold part of the city from 1229 to 1244, but they left virtually no trace of their rule during this period, in contrast to that of the 12th century, when Jerusalem served as the focal point of the Crusades.

Today we know more about this than any other period in the annals of Jerusalem, thanks in the main to the abundance of written sources that have survived from that period: legal and commercial documents, pilgrims' descriptions and accounts, maps drawn by them and for them. Archaeological exploration of Crusader Jerusalem has been expanded in recent years and the resultant finds have added to our knowledge on the subject. Jerusalem fell to the Crusader armies on 15 July 1099 following a siege that lasted more than a month. The besieging forces were divided into five groups: Godfrey of Bouillon and his army encamped in the area of today's Rockefeller Museum near the northeastern corner of the city's northern wall; Robert of Flanders and Robert of Normandy had arrayed their forces on either side of the Damascus Gate along the same wall; Tancred's army was stationed opposite the northwestern corner of the wall (today's Zahal Square); while the men of Provence, led by Raymond of St. Gilles, faced Mount Zion in the southwest.

The breakthrough came in Godfrey's sector, in the area of today's Moslem Quarter. At the point of entry, the invaders implanted a large cross, which remained in place as long as the Crusaders remained in control of the city.

When the city had been taken, the Crusaders massacred its non-Christian inhabitants: the Jews were gathered together in their synagogues and burned alive, while some Moslems were slaughtered and some permitted to leave the city and make their way to Ashkelon or to Damascus, both of which were at that time under Moslem rule. Those evicted were not allowed to return — at least not during the first few years following the conquest of Jerusalem. At the same time, the new rulers of the city saw to it that Jerusalem was re-populated by Christians in various ways: retroactive approval of title deeds to real estate seized by Crusader warriors during the conquest of the city; the importation of Christian Arabs from the border areas of Palestine and Syria and their settlement in the abandoned quarters of the city (whence the appellation 'Syrian' Quarter); and special tax remissions and other concessions.

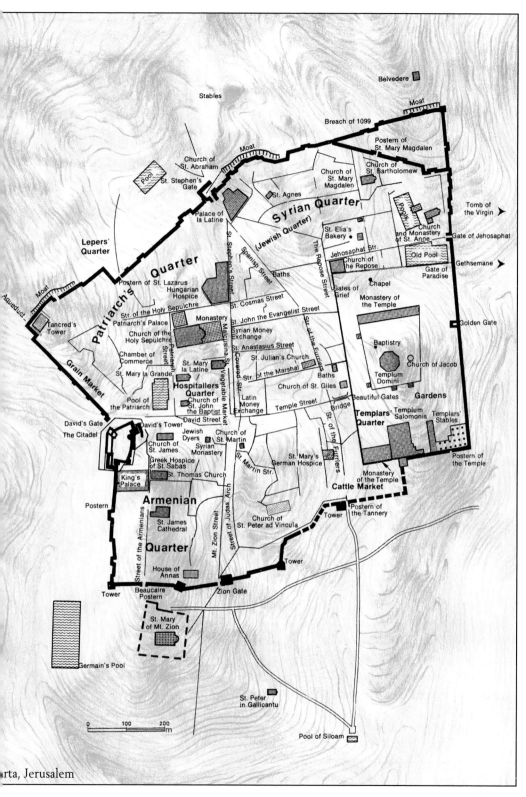

Belvedere

Moat

Stables

Breach of 1099

Postern of
St. Mary Magdalen

Church of
St. Abraham

Moat

Church of
St. Bartholomew

Church of
St. Mary
Magdalen

Pool

Church of St. Stephen's Gate

St. Agnes

Tomb of
the Virgin

Palace of
la Latine

Syrian Quarter

Church
and Monastery
of St. Anne

Gate of Jehosaphat

Lepers'
Quarter

(Jewish Quarter)

St. Elia's
Bakery

Old Pool

Gethsemane

Jehosaphat Str.

Gate of
Paradise

Patriarch's Quarter

Postern of St. Lazarus

Spanish Street

Baths

Church of
the Repose

Chapel

Aqueduct

Moat

Hungarian
Hospice

St. Stephen's Street

Gates of
Grief

Monastery of
the Temple

Str. of the Holy Sepulchre

St. Cosmas Street

Golden Gate

Tancred's
Tower

Patriarch's Palace

Monastery

St. John the Evangelist Street

Church of the
Holy Sepulchre

Malquisinat Str.

Syrian Money
Exchange

Str. of the Furriers

Baptistry

Grain Market

Chamber of
Commerce

St. Anastasius Street

Church of Jacob

St. Mary la Grande

St. Mary
la Latine

Patriarch Street

St. Julian's Church

Str. of the Marshal

Templum
Domini

Vegetable Market

Hospitallers
Quarter

Church of St. Giles

Gardens

Pool of
the Patriarch

Church of
St. John
the Baptist

Covered Str.

Latin
Money
Exchange

Temple Street

Baths

Beautiful Gates

Templum
Salomonis

Templars'
Stables

David's Gate

David's Tower

David Street

Bridge

Templars'
Quarter

The Citadel

Church of
St. James

Jewish
Dyers

Church of
St. Martin

Str. of the Furriers

Postern of
the Temple

Syrian
Monastery

King's
Palace

Greek Hospice
of St. Sabas

St. Mary's
German Hospice

Monastery
of the Temple

St. Thomas Church

St. Martin Str.

Cattle Market

Postern

Armenian

St. James
Cathedral

Church of
St. Peter ad Vincula

Tower

Postern of
the Tannery

Mt. Zion Street

Street of Judas Arch

Quarter

Street of the Armenians

House of
Annas

Tower

Tower

Beaucaire
Postern

Zion Gate

St. Mary
of Mt. Zion

Germain's Pool

St. Peter
in Gallicantu

0   100   200
m

Pool of Siloam

rta, Jerusalem

TURRET ATOP THE DOME OF THE ASCENSION. *This fine example of Crusader art in Jerusalem was a Crusader baptistry which served the Dome of the Rock when the latter was used as a church.*

DEIR ZEITUNA CONVENT *(Convent of the Olive Tree). The convent was so named because it was believed to be the site of the olive tree to which Jesus was tied when brought to trial at the house of the High Priest Annas (John 18: 13). It is also known as the Angels' Convent, to commemorate the appearance of the angels when Jesus was struck by Annas's servant. The present structure dates from the 12th century, with additions made by King Levon III of Armenia.*

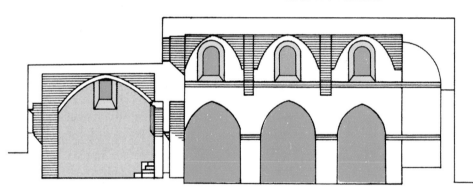

Godfrey of Bouillon was proclaimed ruler of the city. (His official title was Protector of the Holy Sepulchre). The city was also given a Patriarch, to whom was assigned an autonomous quarter of his own - the Patriarch's Quarter, which at that time occupied most of what is today the Christian Quarter. The various Orders also enjoyed semi-independent status: they had so many rights, in fact, that it can almost be said that they were independent of the central Crusader government. They owned considerable property in all parts of the country and beyond, and in Jerusalem too there were places that were under their governance. The Hospitallers had a quarter of their own south of the Church of the Holy Sepulchre; the Templars ruled the Temple Mount (hence their name); and the Teutons occupied what is now the Jewish Quarter. Then there was the Order of St. Lazarus, a small Order whose members devoted themselves to the care of lepers; it administered a leper colony, a monastery and a church — all in the Lepers' Quarter (in the area of today's Notre Dame Convent). All of these Orders enjoyed wide-ranging autonomous authority in their respective quarters.

The wall of Crusader Jerusalem was built along much the same line as the wall that encompasses the city today. Remains of that wall have been uncovered in archaeological excavations conducted at a number of points along its length. At the southern wall, only the vestiges of the western end of the Crusader wall were uncovered, including the remains of five square towers (measuring about 20 x 20 metres). Inscriptions found on these towers point to the Ayyubid period. It would appear, however, that they were only repaired in that era, having been built in an earlier age.

On the western side of the city, the outstanding feature was the Citadel ('Tower of David') with its moat. This fortress, it will be recalled, was in use already a thousand years before the advent of the Crusaders, but it was only in this period that it took on the shape it has preserved to this day: a multi-faceted structure with towers at its corners. The Citadel was surrounded by a moat which existed until the start of the present century, with a drawbridge on its eastern side which was also preserved until then.

Vestiges of the Crusaders' northern wall came to light mainly as a result of the excavations carried out in the Damascus Gate area and in the area of Zahal Square further west. Underneath the Damascus Gate, the remains of the Crusader gate were discovered — actually a double gate, exterior and interior, connected by a wide right-angle passage designed to impede the progress of an invading force. Indeed, this passage was so wide that it was possible to build a small church in its span, known as the Church of St. Abraham.

A moat dug outside the wall was to give added protection to the northern wall at several weak spots: the Bezetha Ridge (in the area of today's Rockefeller Museum), the Antonia Ridge (opposite the Damascus Gate) and the ridge near the northwestern corner of the city wall (Zahal Square). For the further defence of the latter weak point in the northern wall, a high, well-built tower — Tancred's Tower — was erected; its remains still very much in evidence as late as the nineteenth century.

The eastern wall underwent few changes between then and now, the one major difference being in the fact that the Golden Gate was, at that time, opened one day every year, on the Feast of Palm Sunday, for ceremonial purposes. The northeastern corner of the city wall (one of the weak points already mentioned) was reinforced by an inner cross-wall connecting the northern with the eastern wall. Any invader, therefore, who succeeded in penetrating this corner of the city wall found himself up against this second, inner wall which had but one small opening in it — the Postern of St. Mary Magdalen (named after the nearby church of that name). Nothing remains today of this inner wall, though presumably it was built along the Beth Zetha (i.e. Santa Anna) Valley.

Jerusalem of the Crusader era was first and foremost a major Christian religious centre — a fact which largely determined its character and physical shape. The city has an abundance of sites commemorating the lives of Jesus, his family and Disciples; and the faithful came to Jerusalem to visit those places which were marked mainly by churches or memorials. Sometimes a number of memorials would be erected one next to the other, each belonging to a different Christian denomination with a tradition of its own. The various denominations — and sometimes even Christian countries — would each setup a kind of community centre of its own, which usually included a church and a pilgrims' hospice. In the nature of things, the pilgrims who came to Jerusalem came in contact with the local populace, most of them 'Syrians' — local Christians from Palestine and Syria.

There were generally separate markets for the Westerners (Latins) and the Easterners (Syrians). To meet the needs of the pilgrims, facilities such as moneychangers' booths and shops offering religious articles, souvenirs and the like soon sprang up all over the city. The commercial life of Jerusalem was concentrated largely in the heart of the city, in and around the various marketplaces. A few specialized markets were scattered in other parts of the city as well: the grain market, for example, along the northern section of the west

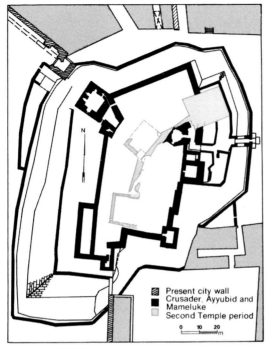

Present city wall
Crusader, Ayyubid and Mameluke
Second Temple period

0 10 20 m

DAMASCUS GATE THROUGH THE AGES. To date the Damascus Gate is the only one of the Turkish gates that has been systematically excavated and explored. Underneath the present structure the foundations of the Crusader gate were discovered, which in turn had followed the lines of an earlier (Roman) model but was better fortified. Entry into the city through this gate was effected not in a straight line but at right angles, as an added restraint on an invading force.

THE CITADEL was designed to guard Jerusalem's weaker western approach. One of its towers (the 'Tower of David') dates to the period of the Second Temple. Ever since a fortress has stood on this site undergoing changes from time to time. Its present shape was fixed during the Crusader period, when the city's governor and his military commanders made it their headquarters. In 1219 the Citadel was partly destroyed by the Mameluke ruler El-Muazzem to be restored in 1247 by El-Malik el-Salih Ayyub. It was again restored in 1310 by Nasser Muhammad Ibn Kalaoun. Finally Turkish Sultan Suleiman the Magnificent added the mosque, the turret and the Citadel's main gate.

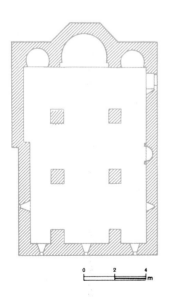

THE CHURCH OF ST. AGNES was a typical Crusader church of the twelfth century. Today it is the the Mosque of Mawlawiyya, in the heart of the Moslem Quarter.

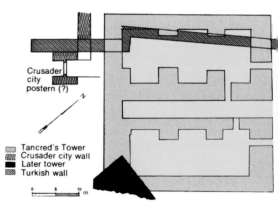

Crusader city postern (?)

Tancred's Tower
Crusader city wall
Later tower
Turkish wall

0 5 10 m

THE TOWER OF GOLIATH is located at the northwestern corner of the city wall. According to Moslem tradition, the tower was believed to be the site of the David—Goliath duel. It is also known as Tancred's Tower after the Crusader prince of that name whose forces were stationed here during the siege of Jerusalem in 1099. It was built during the first half of the twelfth century to protect this weak spot in the city's defences.

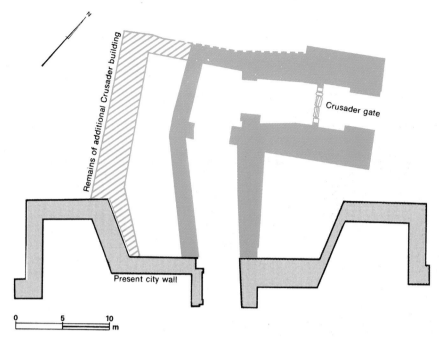

Remains of additional Crusader building

Crusader gate

Present city wall

0   5   10
m

wall, and the cattle market, near the Western ('Wailing') Wall, which included a slaughter-house and a number of furriers' workshops. Other workshops and small industrial enterprises of various kinds were to be found in various places along the city streets. According to a source dated 1167, a number of Jews were then to be found in Jerusalem, living near David's Tower and practising the dyers' trade.

The Temple Mount, taken over by the Templars, was a place of special importance for the Crusaders, as it had been for their forerunners. The Mosque of El-Aqsa, restored and refurbished, and renamed Templum Salomonis' (Solomon's Temple), became the Order's religious centre. The form given the building at that time has come down to us practically unaltered. Nearby, several service structures were put up for the use of members of the Order, among these the Cloister (north of today's Women's Mosque) and Solomon's Stables. Architectural remains of Templar edifices are to be found to this day in the El-Aqsa Mosque and its immediate vicinity.

0   5   10
m

THE ARMENIAN CHURCH OF ST. JAMES stands on the traditional site of the house of James the Less, brother of Jesus, whose remains were brought here for burial in the fourth century. Also buried here, according to Christian tradition, is the head of James the Great (brother of John the Baptist) who was beheaded by Herod Agrippa in the year 44 CE. A church occupied the spot in the fourth century; it is believed that a house of prayer stood here as early as the first century. Destroyed in the Persian invasion in 614, the church was rebuilt in the eighth century. The Crusaders gave it its final form in the twelfth. Since then it has been lavishly embellished by various Armenian patrons and rulers, and today it is the main cathedral of the Armenian community in Jerusalem.

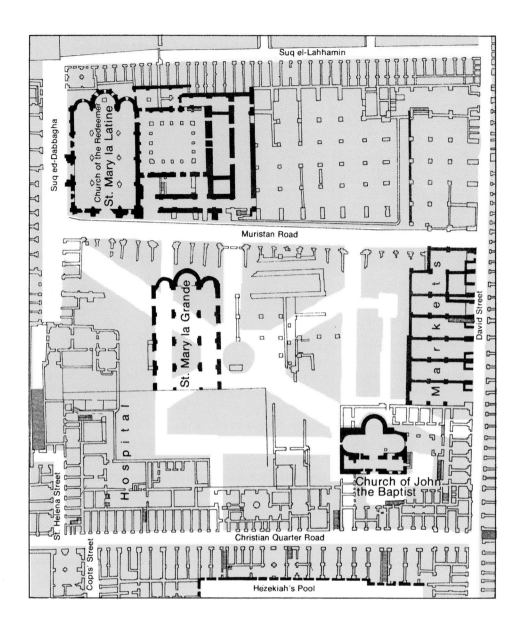

Map labels:

Suq el-Lahhamin

Suq ed-Dabbagha

Church of the Redeemer
St. Mary la Latine

Muristan Road

St. Mary la Grande

Markets

David Street

Hospital

St. Helena Street

Copts' Street

Church of John the Baptist

Christian Quarter Road

Hezekiah's Pool

THE MURISTAN. *Shown here is the district between David Street and the Church of the Holy Sepulchre during the Crusader period. In Roman and Byzantine times, the City Forum was located in this area; when the Crusaders came, centuries later, it was given over to the knights that came to be known as the Knights of St. John, Knights of Rhodes and Malta, or Knights Hospitallers. (They operated a hospital here for visiting pilgrims). The Hospitallers also built a market, monasteries and other buildings in the area. When Saladin captured Jerusalem, his people continued to use the hospital, whence the name of the quarter — Muristan, which is Kurdish for 'hospital.' Later the area fell into disuse and general neglect and in 1869 was given in part to the Germans, who built the Church of the Redeemer on the site of the Crusader Church of St. Mary la Latine. Ownership of the western portion of the Muristan was transferred to the Greeks who in 1905 built their own distinctive commercial area here.*

TOMB OF THE VIRGIN. Part of a Crusader monastery in the Kidron Valley, it is built on the spot where, according to Christian tradition, Mary, mother of Jesus, was buried. It is also the burial site of Queen Melisande, who ruled Jerusalem during the Crusader era.

The Dome of the Rock, further north on the Temple Mount, was turned into the Temple of the Lord — 'Templum Domini.' The Templars refrained from altering the structure of this magnificent building, merely adding a metal guardrail around the sacred rock inside the building. The railing remained in place until it was removed by the Jordanians during their occupation of East Jerusalem between 1948 and 1967. Northwest of the Dome of the Rock the Crusaders erected an elaborate baptistry, named today the Dome of the Ascension. They also used the Dome of the Chain as a shrine to commemorate St. James. In the northern portion of the Temple Mount a monastery was erected to house the monks who served in the area. Other sites in this part of the Mount, such as Solomon's Dome were exhibited in the Crusader period as places connected with Jesus' last journey. Judging from contemporary testimony as well as from structural remains found there, it appears that the Temple Mount was transformed by the Crusaders into a place of distinction and great splendour — a special attraction for Christian pilgrims from near and far — until it returned to Moslem hands following the conquest of Jerusalem by Saladin in 1187.

The general outlines of the Crusader city have been preserved down to the present day. Many of the Crusader buildings continued in use in later periods, and quite a few continue in use to this day.

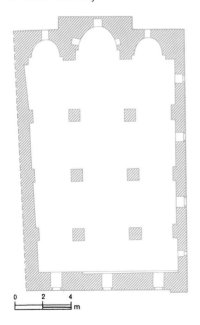

0 2 4
m

CRUSADER CHURCH. A typical plan of a medium-sized Crusader church. It has three apses, where smaller churches (such as St. James or St. Marcus) have but one. Well preserved, this church was discovered only recently, and it is believed to be the Church of St. Julian, mentioned in a contemporary source.

57

THE AYYUBID AND MAMELUKE PERIOD
1187-1517

FOUNTAIN OF QAIT BEY has graced the Temple Mount since 1483. (Nineteenth century copper engraving).

This chapter deals with the history of Jerusalem from its capture by Saladin in 1187 to the Turkish conquest in the year 1517. After Saladin's conquest, the city was ruled by the Ayyubids. Then, for 15 years (1229–1244), part of the city came once more under Christian rule, and in the year 1250 it was taken by the Mamelukes, whose imprint on the city is evident to this day.

Saladin laid siege to Jerusalem for about ten days (21 September to 2 October 1187) and, after negotiating with representatives of its inhabitants, allowed its Christian inhabitants to leave the city unharmed. The Moslem conquerors settled in the newly emptied houses, demolished some of the structures the Crusaders had put up on the Temple Mount, but on the whole spared the city's churches. The Church of St. Anne was converted into a Moslem school named after Saladin, Madrasa Salahiyya. The Church of the Holy Sepulchre was taken over by the Moslems who at first prohibited the Christians from visiting it. In the course of time, however, the ban was lifted as the Moslems learned to turn Christian pilgrimage to their own monetary advantage.

In repairing the city walls, Saladin made use of stones from the monastery that had stood over Mary's Tomb. In his time too, the course of the southern wall was modified somewhat in order to include Mount Zion within its perimeter; a portion of this additional section was discovered during excavations on Mount Zion in the 19th century. The Patriarch's Palace, near the Church of the Holy Sepulchre, became a hostel for Dervishes called Khanqah Salahiyya — a name it has retained to this day. No other major changes were carried out by Saladin after he captured Jerusalem.

From one of the inscriptions found on Mount Zion we learn that subsequent rulers of the Ayyubid dynasty continued through the 13th century to reinforce the city walls. In the year 1219, however, the Ayyubid governor of Damascus, El-Malek Mu'azzam Issa, ordered

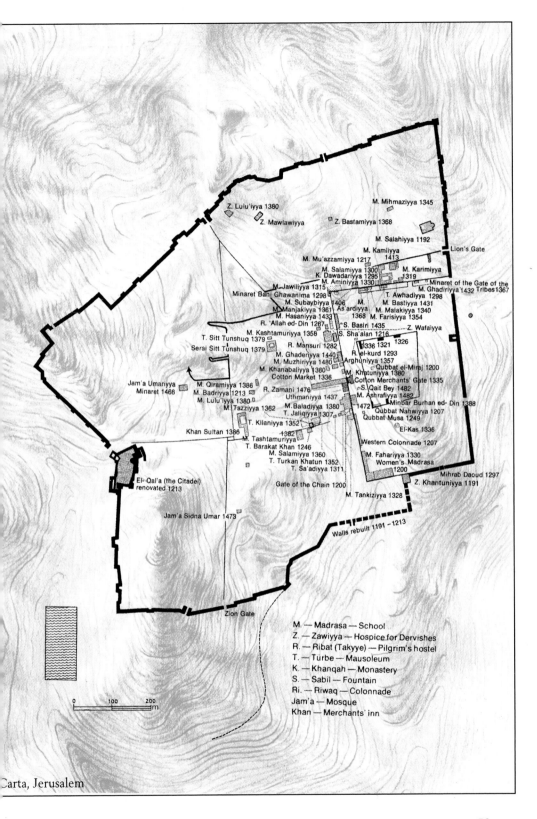

M. Mihmaziyya 1345

Z. Lulu'iyya 1380
Z. Mawlawiyya
Z. Bastamiyya 1368

M. Salahiyya 1192

Lion's Gate

M. Kamliyya 1413

M. Mu'azzamiyya 1217
M. Salamiyya 1300
K. Dawadariyya 1295
M. Aminiyya 1330
M-Jawiliyya 1315
Minaret Bani Ghawanima 1298
M. Subaybiyya
M:Manjakiyya 1361
M. Hasaniyya 1433
R. 'Allah ed-Din 1267
M. Kashtamuriyya 1358
T. Sitt Tunshuq 1379
Serai Sitt Tunshuq 1379
M. Ghaderiyya 1440
M. Muzhiriyya 1480
M. Khanabaliyya 1380
Cotton Market 1336
Jam'a Umariyya
Minaret 1466
M. Qiramiyya 1386
M. Badriyya 1213
M. Lulu'iyya 1380
M. Tazziyya 1362
T. Kilaniyya 1352
Khan Sultan 1386
1382
M. Tashtamuriyya
T. Barakat Khan 1246
M. Salamiyya 1360
T. Turkan Khatun 1352
T. Sa'adiyya 1311
Gate of the Chain 1200

M. Karimiyya
1319
Minaret of the Gate of the
M. Ghadiriyya 1432 Tribes 1367
T. Awhadiyya 1298
M.
As'ardiyya
1368
M. Bastiyya 1431
M. Malakiyya 1340
M. Farisiyya 1354
S. Basiri 1435
Z. Wafaiyya
S. Sha'alan 1216
1336 1321 1326
R. Mansuri 1282
R. el-kurd 1293
Qubbat el-Miraj 1200
Arghuniyya 1357
M. Khatuniyya 1380
R. Zamani 1476
Cotton Merchants' Gate 1335
Uthmaniyya 1437
S. Qait Bey 1482
M. Baladiyya 1380
M. Ashrafiyya 1482
Jaliqiyya 1307
Minbar Burhan ed-Din 1388
1472
Qubbat Nahwiyya 1207
Qubbat Musa 1249
El-Kas 1336
Western Colonnade 1207
M. Fahariyya 1330
Women's Madrasa
1200
Mihrab Daoud 1297
Z. Khantuniyya 1191

M. Tankiziyya 1328

El-Qal'a (the Citadel)
renovated 1213

Jam'a Sidna Umar 1473

Walls rebuilt 1191–1213

Zion Gate

M. — Madrasa — School
Z. — Zawiyya — Hospice for Dervishes
R. — Ribat (Takyye) — Pilgrim's hostel
T. — Türbe — Mausoleum
K. — Khanqah — Monastery
S. — Sabil — Fountain
Ri. — Riwaq — Colonnade
Jam'a — Mosque
Khan — Merchants' inn

0   100   200
m.

Carta, Jerusalem

59

the fortifications of Jerusalem demolished. As a result, many of the city's inhabitants left, and its importance declined sharply. The destruction of the city's defences was bemoaned by those who remained loyal to Jerusalem. Deeply resented in particular was the demolition of the Citadel (David's Tower) which, for generations upon generations, had been the pride of Jerusalem's defence perimeter. It was not until about a hundred years later (about 1310) that Nasser Muhammad Ibn Kalaoun rebuilt the Citadel, which except for a few additions has not undergone any modifications since then. The city walls on the other hand, continued for many more years to lie in ruins, to be restored only in the years 1536-1539 by the Turkish Sultan Suleiman the Magnificent.

At the start of the Mameluke period, Jerusalem was of minor importance politically. It was part of the Syrian province, whose capital was Damascus, and it was the governors of Damascus who were responsible for its administration. Inscriptions on buildings of that period show that they were built at the behest of the governors of Damascus. A change in this situation came about in the year 1376. Its status was raised, and its governor was appointed directly by Cairo, the Mameluke capital. A new chapter was inaugurated in the annals of Jerusalem which found expression, among other things, in the construction of a large number of beautiful buildings all over the city, but especially on the Temple Mount and in its vicinity. Each of the Mameluke rulers made a point of restoring and refurbishing existing structures on the Mount or erecting new ones. For example, Tankiz, Governor of Damascus, arranged to bring the waters of Solomon's Pools, high in the Judean hills south of Jerusalem, to the drinking water installation situated on the Temple Mount between the two big shrines. Qait Bey built a magnificent fountain on the Temple Mount, as well as the Madrasa nearby — one of the finest edifices on the Mount. Many of these structures (the builders' names often inscribed on them) have been preserved down to our day.

Much of our information on Mameluke Jerusalem is based on the detailed descriptions of the contemporary Jerusalem jurist, Mujir ed-Din, contained in a book written by him and published in 1495. These descriptions have enabled us to obtain a fairly accurate picture of the city in those days. The Temple Mount was still the heart and core of Jerusalem, radiating its aura of holiness throughout the city. Theologians and religious functionaries from Islamic countries came to Jerusalem to study, and for them a number of religious academies, or madrasas, were built on the Temple Mount or nearby. For needy Moslem pilgrims who came to Jerusalem to worship at its holy places, hostels were constructed in various parts of the city. Among the public buildings erected in Jerusalem at that time was the Dar en-Niabeh, originally called Jawiliyya — a madrasa later converted into the governor's residence. (It was built where the Antonia Fortress had once stood).

Several new markets were added to Jerusalem during the Mameluke period, the best-known among them being the cotton market, established by the Syrian governor Tankiz in 1336. The city's fountains and other water supply installations underwent repair and embellishment on several occasions in the course of this era, especially under Kalaoun and under Qait Bey.

Outside the city walls, too, a number of buildings were erected, among them the Khan ed-Daher, an impressive structure housing a flour-mill and a bakery, that was built in the reign of the Sultan Baibars in the year 1263. The gates of the structure, brought to Jerusalem from the Government Palace in Cairo, were adorned by two stone-embossed lions — later to be transferred to St. Stephen's Gate in the eastern wall which came to be known as the Lions' Gate. Also erected (or restored) outside the walls, in what is today

TOMB OF UZBEK WOMAN. *The memorial plaque and tomb date from the 14th century. Situated in the Street of the Chain.*

MADRASA ASHRAFIYYA. *This beautiful Mameluke facade was built in the 15th century on the Temple Mount.*

the Abu-Tor district, was a structure named after the Sheikh Abu-Tor, who fought alongside Saladin when Jerusalem was captured in 1187. Among the sites beyond the walls mention might be made of the three major cemeteries of the city: Mamilla in the west, Adhamiyya in the north and the cemetery on the eastern slope of the Temple Mount in the vicinity of the Golden Gate. The Jewish cemetery, dating from the Second Temple period, was located on the Mount of Olives, directly to the east of Jerusalem. The Jewish community, severely decimated in the Crusader conquest of Jerusalem, came to life again during the Mameluke era, being concentrated mainly in what remains to this day the Jewish Quarter. Throughout this period, Jews from various countries came to Jerusalem and settled there. In 1267, the renowned Bible commentator, Nahmanides, came to Jerusalem and built a synagogue in the heart of the Jewish Quarter. In the 14th century, Estori Ha-Parhi, author of the first geography book in the Hebrew language, Kaftor va-Ferah, made his home in Jerusalem. Numerous Christian pilgrims made a point of mentioning, in their travel accounts, that their guides in Jerusalem were Jews, who were known to be familiar with the city's sites and its places of historical and religious interest.

Growing attention was focused during this period on Mount Zion. According to Christian

MAMELUKE MAUSOLEUM. In addition to the Mameluke cemeteries uncovered within the city area, graves of that period were found also in cemeteries outside the walls. The best-known of these in the Mamilla Cemetery, adjacent to the Mamilla Pool. Use of the site as a graveyard goes back to the Crusader era; under the Mamelukes, it became the city's main cemetery. Depicted here is the Kebakiyya, one of the grandest mausoleums found in this cemetery. It marks the burial-place of Allah ed-Din el-Kebaki, whose date of demise is recorded as being 23 September 1289. The structure of this grave may include elements taken from a Crusader church that is believed to have stood on this spot.

THE TANKIZIYYA (El-Mahkama). Located opposite the Gate of the Chain, in a characteristically medieval courtyard, the building is surrounded by other Mameluke structures. Erected originally as a school by Seif ed-Din Tankiz in 1329, it was soon converted into the city's civil law court, which it remained until the end of the Turkish period; hence its other name — al-Mahkama (law court). Jewish tradition has it that this is the site of the Chamber of Hewn Stone, the seat of the Sanhedrin in Second Temple times. Under the Jordanians (1948-1967), the building was used as a secondary school.

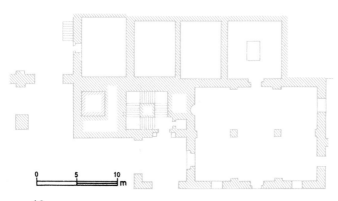

THE ASHRAFIYYA. This school, on the Temple Mount, was built by the Emir Hassan ed-Dahari and later handed over to Qait Bey. For a time it housed dignitaries of the Sufi sect. Demolished in 1475, the school was rebuilt in 1482. One of the finest examples of Mameluke architecture in Jerusalem, the Ashrafiyya was, in its time, considered the third-most beautiful building on the Temple Mount.

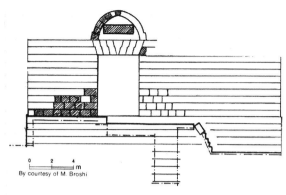

RESTORED GATE-TOWER. Remains of this gate-tower were discovered east of Zion Gate. An inscription found nearby fixes the construction date at 1212, when El-Malek el-Mu'azzam ruled the realm. Seven years later, this ruler had the tower and other fortifications demolished, to forestall the possibility of the Crusaders returning to Jerusalem and using these structures as a shelter. The tower measured approximately 20 by 20 metres. There are known to have been four additional towers in the southern wall; the one depicted here was probably a replacement for the Roman gate at the southern end of the Cardo. It may also be identified with the Nea Gate of the early Arab period.

tradition, a number of events connected with the lives of Jesus and his disciples, among them the Last Supper, took place on this mountain. In the Crusader period, an Armenian church was built on Mount Zion, known to this day as Caiaphas' House. The Church of Mount Zion was razed to the ground by El-Malek Mu'azzam Issa and not rebuilt. In the first half of the 14th century, Mount Zion was procured by the Franciscans, who erected the Church of the Last Supper (1342) and, near it, the Franciscan Monastery (1352). In 1490 the Christians were expelled from the mountain, only to return a short time later. After being driven from it a second time, however, in 1552, they were unable to return until quite recently. Indeed, the last two centuries of Mameluke rule were marked by constant intercommunal rivalries and conflict over control of the mountain and its sites. Often the Jews were accused of expelling the Christians from Mount Zion on the grounds that this was the site of David's Tomb.

In 1260, when the Mongolian invasion was repulsed by the Mamelukes, quiet reigned within the Mameluke kingdom. At this time Jerusalem was almost entirely Moslem; only minimal numbers of Christians remained in the city. But their numbers slowly increased, enjoying the favour of the influential Christian countries. According to Obadiah of Bertinoro, who came to Jerusalem in 1488, some 200 Jewish families resided in the city. Jerusalem, at the time, was indeed a backwater and was often a last resort for princes and ministers who had fallen from favour, retired army officers and even 'wayward' women.

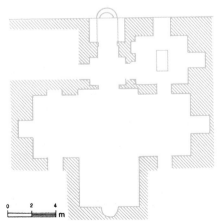

THE ARGHUNIYYA. This religious academy was completed in 1358, a year after the death of its originator, Arghun ef-Kamali, governor of Syria, buried here in October 1357. It is located in one of the most interesting streets in the Old City of Jerusalem, the Street of the Iron Gate, which to this day retains its medieval appearance. It contains several school buildings and mausoleums, all in the ornamental style that prevailed in the region during the Mameluke era.

THE TURKISH PERIOD
1517 -1917

THE CITADEL. This western view shows the turret of the Turkish mosque atop the Tower of David.

Towards the end of the year 1516, a pitched battle took place between the armies of the Turkish Sultan Selim I and of the Mameluke ruler, Qansuh el-Ghori, at Marj Dabek, near Aleppo, in which the Sultan Selim emerged the victor. This military triumph paved the way for the Turks to conquer all of Palestine, including Jerusalem. When the Sultan entered Jerusalem on 30 December 1516, the city's inhabitants welcomed him with open arms, and Selim I celebrated his victory on the Temple Mount. As his first act he distributed money to the needy. Thus began the Turkish period in the annals of Jerusalem, which ended in 1917, when the British captured the city towards the end of the First World War.

In the early years of the Turkish conquest the city remained as neglected as it had been in the Mameluke eta. However, after the Sultan Suleiman the Magnificent (1520-1566) returned from his wars of conquest in Europe, he decided to consolidate his rule in Jerusalem. With this end in view, he began refortifying the city — the first time in three hundred years. The rebuilding of the city walls was begun in 1536. Archaeological studies show that the Turkish builders followed the previous line of the wall, making use of whatever building materials came to hand — from the hewn stone of Herod's day to the ordinary rocks and stones used in earlier periods. Similarly, they restored its ancient gates: the Damascus Gate and the Jaffa Gate. Presumably, it was at this time that the Golden Gate, the Single Gate and the Triple Gate, in the Temple Mount wall, were finally sealed.

On the city's southern flank, the wall, which had been moved several times in the course of the centuries, was rebuilt on the foundations of the old southern wall (as it was called in the late Roman and again in the Crusader period). The location of the Zion Gate was altered to facilitate the approach to Mount Zion and the Tomb of David. Incidentally, the presence of the Franciscan Order in this area, considered one of the city's weak spots

64

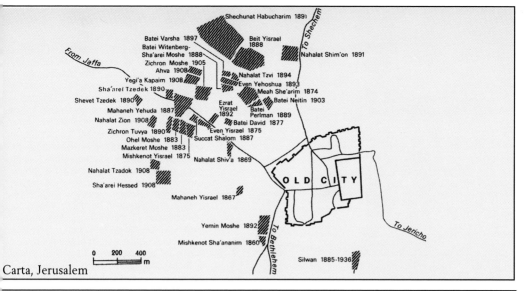

Shechunat Habucharim 1891
Batei Varsha 1897
Beit Yisrael 1888
Batei Witenberg-
Sha'arei Moshe 1888
Zichron Moshe 1905
Ahva 1908
Yegi'a Kapaim 1908
Sha'arei Tzedek 1890
Shevet Tzedek 1890
Mahaneh Yehuda 1887
Nahalat Zion 1908
Zichron Tuvya 1890
Ohel Moshe 1883
Mazkeret Moshe 1883
Mishkenot Yisrael 1875
Nahalat Tzadok 1908
Sha'arei Hessed 1908
Mahaneh Yisrael 1867

Nahalat Shim'on 1891
Nahalat Tzvi 1894
Even Yehoshua 1893
Meah She'arim 1874
Batei Neitin 1903
Ezrat Yisrael 1892
Batei Perlman 1889
Batei David 1877
Even Yisrael 1875
Succat Shalom 1887
Nahalat Shiv'a 1869

To Shechem
Nahalat Shim'on 1891

OLD CITY

To Jericho

Yemin Moshe 1892
Mishkenot Sha'ananim 1860
To Bethlehem
Silwan 1885-1936

From Jaffa

0 200 400
m

Carta, Jerusalem

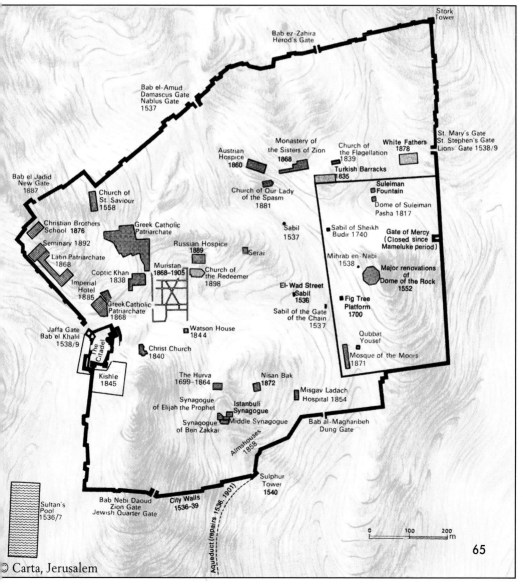

Stork Tower

Bab ez-Zahira
Herod's Gate

Bab el-Amud
Damascus Gate
Nablus Gate
1537

St. Mary's Gate
St. Stephen's Gate
Lions' Gate 1538/9

Monastery of
the Sisters of Zion
1868
Church of
the Flagellation
1839
White Fathers
1878

Austrian Hospice
1860
Turkish Barracks
1835

Bab el Jadid
New Gate
1887

Suleiman Fountain

Church of
St. Saviour
1558

Church of Our Lady
of the Spasm
1881

Dome of Suleiman
Pasha 1817

Christian Brothers
School 1876

Sabil
1537
Sabil of Sheikh
Budir 1740

Gate of Mercy
(Closed since
Mameluke period)

Greek Catholic
Patriarchate

Seminary 1892

Russian Hospice
1889

Mihrab en-Nabi
1538

Latin Patriarchate
1868

Serai

Major renovations
of
Dome of the Rock
1552

Coptic Khan
1838

Muristan
1868-1905
Church of
the Redeemer
1898

El-Wad Street
1536

Imperial
Hotel
1885

Sabil
Fig Tree
Platform
1700

Greek Catholic
Patriarchate
1868

Sabil of the Gate
of the Chain
1537

Jaffa Gate
Bab el Khalil
1538/9

The Citadel

Watson House
1844

Qubbat
Yousef

Kishle
1845

Christ Church
1840

Mosque of the Moors
1871

The Hurva
1699-1864

Nisan Bak
1872

Misgav Ladach
Hospital 1854

Synagogue
of Elijah the Prophet

Istanbuli
Synagogue

Synagogue
of Ben Zakkai

Middle Synagogue

Bab al-Magharibeh
Dung Gate

Almshouses
1858

Sultan's
Pool
1536/7

Bab Nebi Daoud
Zion Gate
Jewish Quarter Gate

City Walls
1536-39

Sulphur
Tower
1540

Aqueduct (repairs 1536, 1901)

0 100 200
m

65

© Carta, Jerusalem

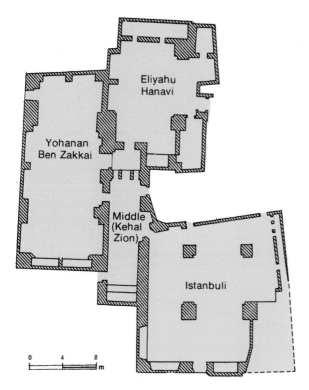

Eliyahu
Hanavi

Yohanan
Ben Zakkai

Middle
(Kehal
Zion)

Istanbuli

0   4   8
—————————
m

THE SEPHARDIC SYNAGOGUES.
*Following the Turkish conquest of Palestine,
Jews, descended from the Spanish exiles
of 1492 who had previously settled in
Turkey, began arriving in Jerusalem.
The complex of four synagogues which
they built here became the centre of the
Spanish-Jewish (Sephardic) community in
Jerusalem. The complex is known as the
Yohanan Ben Zakkai Synagogue, though
each of its four component parts has its
own separate name. It was destroyed
during the Jordanian occupation (1948-
1967) and restored in 1972, after the
reunification of the city. The synagogues
clearly reveal their architectural origins,
particularly the one named 'Istanbuli,'
which is reminiscent of Turkish buildings
of the period: a square structure, with four
central pillars supporting the domed roof.
The Ben Zakkai Synagogue is believed to
have been constructed on the ruins of a
Crusader church; an unusual feature is
its twin Holy Arks in the front wall of the
cham-ber. The Eliyahu Hanavi Synagogue,
built in the same style as the Istanbuli, has
preserved certain traditional relics, such
as the chair popularly believed to have
been used by the Prophet Elijah. The
Middle Synagogue is a later addition,
constructed to fill the space left between
the larger synagogues.*

strategically, was viewed by the new rulers with a jaundiced eye, and in 1552 the Franciscans were evicted from Mount Zion and their institutions relocated to the northwestern
corner of the city, where they are to be found to this day.

Architecturally, the restoration of the walls of Jerusalem by Suleiman the Magnificent is
considered a major feat, since there are not many places where the Turks built fortifications
of this kind and took pains to embellish them with all manner of adornments. As defensive
bastions on the other hand, their efficacy may be called into question. Apparently, Suleiman's wall was designed mainly to protect the city from inroads by marauding Bedouin
from the surrounding desert and possibly against local uprisings. They were not formidable
enough, however, to withstand the massed onslaught of a fully-fledged invading army.

While the wall project was, without doubt, Suleiman's greatest achievement in Jerusalem,
it was preceded by another project initiated by the Sultan: assuring Jerusalem of a regular
and adequate supply of water — always a topline challenge to the rulers of this city. The
aqueduct from Solomon's Pools to Jerusalem was repaired, and six fountains were constructed within the city to receive the waters. Inscriptions found on these installations
indicate that the work was begun in the year 1532. Parts of earlier structures built by the
Crusaders were used by the Turks to embellish these fountains. This admixture of Crusader
and Turkish architecture created a new and unique building style, characteristic of the city
of Jerusalem, where east and west did meet (Rudyard Kipling notwithstanding) and do to
this day.

In spite of these enterprises designed to promote the welfare and development of Jerusalem, a decided decline in the city's fortunes set in a short time later. Its population

CITY GATES. Most of the gates to be found today in the Old City wall were built after the Turkish conquest, over 400 years ago. The Lions' Gate, Jaffa Gate, Damascus Gate and several others were erected on precisely the same spot where the city gates had been in Roman times — a notable exception being the Zion Gate. These gates represent a unique example of 16th century Turkish civic architecture, with its rosette decorations and its historical and religious inscriptions in ornamental frames. To forestall the quick entry of an invading force, all the gates were constructed so as to create an angular entranceway. Some have been widened in more recent times to allow the passage of vehicular traffic.

decreased, the condition of the roads deteriorated and water and drainage systems fell into disrepair. The decline which continued for centuries, has been linked by some to the discovery of the route to India — an event that relegated the Near East to the status of a kind of backyard of the Turkish Empire. The Turkish government paid little heed to what was happening in Palestine in general, and in Jerusalem in particular, and Jerusalem was the worse for it. The governors of the city obtained their position by bribery and spent their terms of office trying to recover their outlay with as large a profit margin as possible. Pilgrims were ordered to pay a tax upon entering the city, as well as at each one of its historical and religious sites. With the governor and his cohorts pocketing these and other revenues, no funds were available for public purposes. Jerusalem gradually sank into a state of neglect, and many of its inhabitants abandoned the city. The governor, residing at the Jawiliyya, ruled the city with the aid of a small garrison armed with thirty cannon stationed in the Citadel. This was the only outward sign that Jerusalem was part of a great empire.

Christian sources of the 16th century and later provide us with an abundance of information on Jerusalem in this period. From these reports we learn, for example, that many of the churches of Jerusalem frequently changed hands among the various Christian denominations. Occasionally, there would be a spurt of activity on the Temple Mount as this or that Sultan decided to repair or restore some of its structures. For all practical purposes, however, Jerusalem ceased to develop and grow from about the middle of the 17th to the middle of the 19th century. In the pilgrim literature Jerusalem is described as a ghost-town, underpopulated, and with much of its area turned into deserted fields. Well into the 19th century, Jerusalem continued to present a dreary, cheerless aspect. Its streets were narrow and unpaved, and those making their way along them encountered broken stones and raised clouds of dust. In 1808 fire destroyed much of the Church of the Holy Sepulchre. And in 1825 the city was ravaged in the revolt of the Bedouin, which was put down with much brutality.

THE CHURCH OF MARY MAGDALENE.
Beginning in the days of Muhammad Ali's rule, various European powers were granted rights in the country in general, and in Jerusalem in particular. The powers made use of these rights by purchasing plots of land and putting up buildings of various kinds. The first to settle beyond the city walls of Jerusalem were the Russians, who in 1860 founded what came to be known as the Russian Compound (a group of buildings including hostels, a hospital and other facilities designed to cater to pilgrim visitors to Jerusalem). In 1890, at the behest of Czar Alexander III, the Russians erected another structure outside the city walls, the Church of Mary Magdalene on the western slope of the Mount of Olives, facing the Old City. Other powers soon followed suit, putting up buildings in the vicinity of the city. At the same time, the Jewish community also expanded beyond the Old City but the residential quarters built by the Jews were not isolated buildings.

A turning point in the fortunes of Jerusalem came during the reign of the Egyptian Muhammad Ali and his son Ibrahim Pasha (1831-1840). Contrary to the expectations of the local populace, their rule offered no relief to its oppressive predecessors, which accounts for the uprising, in 1834, against Muhammad Ali. Nevertheless, a new reality came into being in Jerusalem during that period — a reality that was to remain even after the city was recaptured by the Turks: for the first time in centuries, a strong central rule was imposed on Jerusalem, and while its inhabitants continued to suffer from a variety of repressive measures, the city as such did enjoy an unprecedented degree of law and order. The number of its inhabitants gradually grew (11,000 in 1838, as against 8,000 in 1806). The non-Moslem population was granted equal rights to the Moslems and for the first time non-Moslems were members of the municipal council. It was at this time, too, that foreign consulates and Christian missions took up residence in Jerusalem. (The British Consulate was opened in 1838).

Perhaps more than anything else, the opening of foreign consulates in Jerusalem paved the way to the city's development. Under a system of granting concessions ('capitulations') to foreign powers, foreign companies were able to invest in building projects throughout the Turkish Empire, including Jerusalem. A railroad was built to the city, and within the city itself roads were paved and various services inaugurated, such as postal agencies, schools, medical clinics and research institutes. Scholars and members of the free professions began to arrive in Palestine — with Jerusalem as their usual destination. With the consulates extending their protection and services to Jews as well, there was a marked growth in the Jewish population of Jerusalem: if, at the start of the 19th century, the Jews constituted but one-fourth of the city's population, by mid-century they were about one-half, growing rapidly, in the years that followed, to 60-70 percent of the total.

All of these changes were reflected also in the appearance of the city, especially so in the latter half of the 19th century. The streets were systematically cleaned and paved with

THE CITADEL GATE. Constructed by Suleiman the Magnificent, as the inscription upon it testifies, this gate and the turret of the mosque were the most important additions to the Citadel in the Turkish period. In the accompanying picture, drawn in 1865, note the Turkish soldiers guarding the entrance to this ancient fortress. The wooden drawbridge seen in the background was removed later by the British, during the Mandate era, and replaced by the concrete bridge that has remained to this day.

stone (1864-5), and gas lighting was installed (1868). In many of the city's streets, water and sewage pipes were laid. The camel, a long-time impediment to pedestrian traffic in the streets, was barred from the city. Building activity by Europeans was encouraged and, beginning about the middle of the 19th century, it grew apace: more churches and hospices were erected, as were post offices, banks, hospitals, hotels and so on. From time to time as the need arose, repairs were effected in the city wall and its gates. The Citadel continued to serve as the base and headquarters of the military unit assigned to defend

PUBLIC FOUNTAIN at Gate of the Chain - one of six erected in Jerusalem by Suleiman the Magnificent.

ARABIC INSCRIPTION from David's Tower. It is similar in style to others found on the walls and towers, and they are all dedicated to Suleiman the Great.

the city, and entry was forbidden except to those who had 'business' there. In 1875 Herod's Gate was reopened; and in 1889 a new gate (known to this day as the 'New Gate') was installed in the northern wall, between the Damascus Gate and its northwestern corner, in order to open a direct, quick route between the Convent of Notre Dame and the Russian Compound outside the Old City, and the Church of the Holy Sepulchre and the Christian Quarter within.

A new development in the history of Jerusalem came in the 1860's. With the rapid growth of the Jewish population, Jews began to establish residential neighbourhoods outside the Old City walls. They were not the first to leave the Old City — the Russians had preceded them to what came to be known as the Russian Compound. The Christians, however, had up to that point restricted themselves, in going beyond the Old City walls, to the construction of hostels and religious and educational institutions, whereas the Jews established fully-fledged residential districts and thus contributed substantially to the growth and development of Jerusalem. Several Christian neighbourhoods followed in their wake (such as the American and German Colonies) as well as Moslem ones (such as the districts established north of Herod's Gate).

The Jews built wherever they were able to buy land, while the Christians strove, as far as possible, to settle near places associated with the history of their faith. The need to stick together as a community, which had characterized the Jewish community within the Old City, determined also the form of Jewish settlement beyond the walls. Thus it transpired that a block of Jewish neighbourhoods came into being between Nablus Road and Jaffa Road, and southwest of Jaffa Road. This block of Jewish residential suburbs became the nucleus of the new city, to which the centre of gravity now shifted.

While it is true that in the course of time the Old City of Jerusalem lost its centrality, it never lost its very special historical, religious and cultural character, which remains intact to this day.

THE RUSSIAN COMPOUND, a complex of buildings established by the Russians to provide services for Russian pilgrims visiting Jerusalem. It was acquired in 1858 and dedicated in 1860. The compound was surrounded by a wall with several gates and inside were the Russian consulate, hospice, hostel etc. Outside the walls, in nearby streets, were other buildings owned by the Russians.

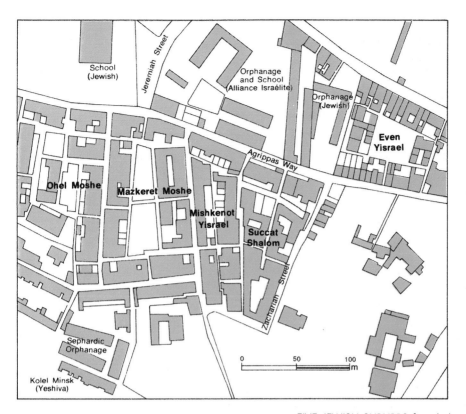

FIVE JEWISH SUBURBS founded next to Rehov Agrippas of today; they are 1. Even Yisrael, 1875; 2. Mishkenot Yisrael, 1875; 3. Mazkeret Moshe, 1883; 4. Ohel Moshe, 1883; 5. Succat Shalom, 1887. Their arrangement around one or more courtyards is typical of the first Jewish suburbs outside the city walls, and they differ from the Christian suburbs in being residential areas rather than religious institutions.

SUNDIAL built in 1906 on Rehov Yafo opposite Mahane Yehuda so that early risers would know the time for prayer. The building housed the Zaharei Hama Synagogue as well as a guest house.

71

THE BRITISH MANDATE
1917-1948

THE SCOTTISH CHURCH. This church was built in a style thought by its designers to be suited to a city where east met west. The church was built in 1927 in memory of the Scottish soldiers who fell in the conquest of Palestine during World War I.

On 11 December 1917 General Allenby entered Jerusalem at the head of his army and the thirty-year period of British rule in Palestine and Jerusalem began. The military administration that operated in the area during the first few years after the capture of Jerusalem was replaced in 1922 by a civilian administration, under the terms of the mandate bestowed upon Britain by the League of Nations. Jerusalem became the centre of British government in Palestine. Britain also saw her role to be the restorer of Christian rule to the city. One of the first acts of the British administration was to set up the Pro-Jerusalem Society whose purpose was to restore neglected buildings and to preserve the special character of the city.

The administration was headed by the High Commissioner, whose headquarters initially were located in the German hospice of Augusta Victoria, on the Mount of Olives. When this building was damaged in the earthquake of 1927, the Commissioner moved to temporary quarters, until a permanent residence was constructed for him which came to be known as Government House (1931) and which continued to serve as the home and headquarters of British High Commissioners until the end of the Mandate period. The city's affairs were in the hands of a council whose members were appointed by the British authorities. Notwithstanding the fact that the majority of the inhabitants of Jerusalem were Jews, the mayor of the city was appointed from among the influential Arab families. The Municipal Council was composed of six Jews and six Arabs (four Moslems and two Christians).

Settlement of Jews beyond the Old City walls, which had begun in the second half of the previous century, continued apace under the British. The year 1922 saw the founding of two new neighbourhoods — Beit Hakerem in the west, and Talpiot in the south. These were to be followed by many others. The Jews of the Old City began to move, in considerable numbers, to the new neighbourhoods to the west.

At the end of the Turkish period some 14,000 inhabitants were crowded into the Jewish Quarter of the Old City of Jerusalem; by 1931 their number had dwindled to 5,600; and

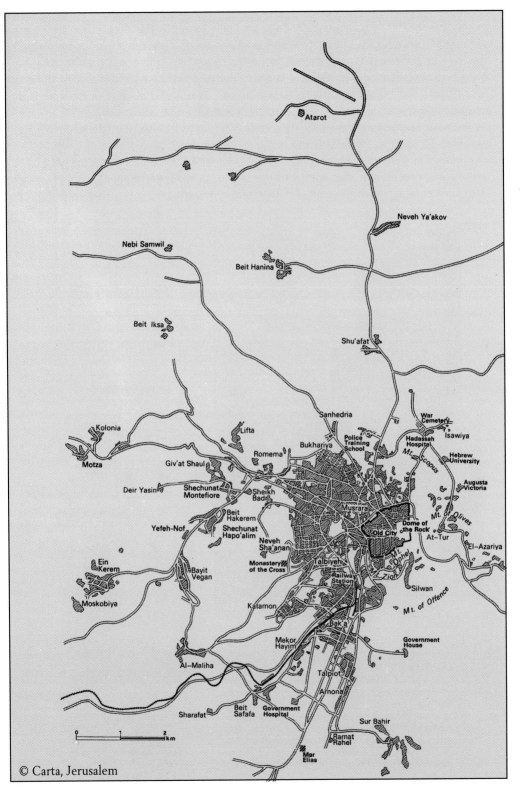

Atarot

Neveh Ya'akov

Nebi Samwil

Beit Hanina

Beit Iksa

Shu'afat

Sanhedria

War Cemetery

Kolonia

Lifta

Police Training School

Hadassah Hospital

Isawiya

Bukhariya

Romema

Mt. Scopus

Hebrew University

Motza

Giv'at Shaul

Augusta Victoria

Deir Yasin

Shechunat Montefiore

Sheikh Badr

Musrara

Yefeh-Nof

Beit Hakerem

Shechunat Hapo'alim

Neveh Sha'anan

Old City

Dome of the Rock

Mt. Olives

At-Tur

El-Azariya

Ein Kerem

Bayit Vegan

Monastery of the Cross

Talbiyeh

Mt. Ophel

Mt. Zion

Moskobiya

Railway Station

Silwan

Katamon

Mt. of Offence

Bak'a

Government House

Mekor Hayim

Al-Maliha

Talpiot

Arnona

Sharafat

Beit Safafa

Government Hospital

Sur Bahir

Ramat Rahel

Mar Elias

0   1   2 km

© Carta, Jerusalem

by the time the British Mandate came to an end only a mere 2,000 were left. In the course of the years, government offices, foreign consulates, schools and other institutions also left the Old City and re-established themselves in the new. The Arabs, too, began to leave the walled city, establishing new residential neighbourhoods in the northern part of the city, near Herod's Gate and in the Sheikh Jarrah Quarter, as well as a number of elegant neighbourhoods in the south, such as Bak'a, Talbiyeh and Katamon.

As Jerusalem expanded, the adequate supply of water to its inhabitants became a major problem. To meet the needs of the resident British army, a pipeline had been laid to channel water from Solomon's Pools to Jerusalem. In 1924 the British authorities built a water-conveying system making use of the springs in Wadi Kelt near Jericho; ten years later they completed another project that brought waters from the Yarkon springs at

GENERAL ALLENBY'S ADDRESS. Britain's General Allenby, standing at the entrance to the Citadel addresses representatives of the local population.

BRITISH MEMORIAL erected in Romema, on the northwestern outskirts of Jerusalem, at the spot where the last Turkish mayor of the city, Hussein Selim el-Husseini, handed the flag of surrender to the British commander. The inscription on the monument reads: "Near this spot the Holy City was surrendered to the 60th London Division, 9th December 1917. Erected by their comrades to those officers, NCOs and men who fell in fighting for Jerusalem."

VIEW OF THE TOWN CENTRE. Here the major government buildings were located and fortified by the British towards the end of the Mandate period. The area was popularly known as 'Bevingrad.' The architecture of these buildings is typical of the period.

Rosh Ha'ayin in the coastal plain up to Jerusalem.

The commercial centre of Jerusalem too, shifted from the markets of the Old City mainly to the nearby eastern section of Jaffa Road and several adjacent streets. This trend was encouraged by the British administration choosing this area to set up its government offices, police headquarters, law courts, the main post office, the radio broadcasting station and so on — a policy that facilitated the defence of these institutions with the outbreak of unrest in 1946, leading to the War of Independence. This fortified British zone (called 'Bevingrad' by the Jews, after the somewhat unpopular British Foreign Minister, Ernest Bevin) served for a while as a buffer between the Jewish commercial centre in the west, and the largely Arab controlled commercial centre in the Mamilla area.

For various reasons, there was no heavy industry in Jerusalem during the British era. The city's inhabitants earned their livelihood mainly from commerce, small industry, crafts and artisanship, services, teaching, and clerical positions (in the government and the Jewish Agency) —a fact that was clearly discernible in the special character of Jerusalem's population.

The British era saw the establishment, in Jerusalem, of institutions as varied as they were numerous, both in the Jewish and in the Arab sector. A major event early on was the founding of the Hebrew University on Mount Scopus, followed, a few years later, by the opening of the large, modern Hadassah Hospital on the same hilltop, in 1932, the Jewish Agency compound was inaugurated in the new Jewish suburb of Rehavia. Jerusalem, which until then had been a religious and cultural centre for the members of the three major faiths, was rapidly being transformed into a national-political centre for two peoples — the Jews and the Arabs.

From time to time, Arab political extremists would launch attacks against the Jewish population in various parts of the country. Often these attacks would take a particularly severe form in the holy city itself. Such attacks and riots broke out in 1920 and again in 1929, from 1936 to 1939 and on the eve of the War of Independence, in 1947-48.

By the end of the British Mandate, the population of Jerusalem had reached 165,000 — 100,000 of these were Jews, 40,000 Moslems and 25,000 Christians. For all practical purposes, Jerusalem was divided into two zones, one Jewish and the other Arab, even before the UN partition resolution of 29 November 1947. Clashes and fighting between these two zones was a common occurrence, and normal contact between the two sectors became less and less — until the outbreak of the War of Independence, which had a profound impact on the shape and character of the city from that time forward.

JERUSALEM DIVIDED
1948 -1967

On 29 November 1947 the General Assembly of the United Nations adopted a resolution calling for the partition of Palestine into a Jewish and an Arab state, and for the internationalization of Jerusalem. The resolution was accepted by the Jews but rejected by the Arabs, who at once opened hostilities against the Jewish community in Palestine. Once again, Jewish Jerusalem was subjected to siege, famine and devastation.

When the British army left the country and the Jewish State of Israel was proclaimed (14 May 1948), the Arab armies invaded Israel, and the Arab Legion - the army of Transjordan - entered the Old City of Jerusalem and captured the eastern part of the city. The inhabitants of the Jewish Quarter were taken prisoner, and much of the Quarter itself, particularly its numerous synagogues and houses of learning, was demolished. Of the entire eastern section of the city, Israel retained control only of the Mount Scopus enclave which included the Hebrew University and the Hadassah Hospital - both now virtually cut off from the rest of Israel and thus rendered useless and desolate: a state of affairs that was to continue until 1967.

In the course of the 1948 fighting, the two sides agreed (on- 22 July 1948) to the demarcation of a no-man's land of varying width that was to serve as a kind of buffer between the Jordan-controlled and Israel-controlled zones of the city. On 30 November a ceasefire was agreed upon which went into effect on 3 April 1949, under the terms of the Armistice Agreement between Israel and Jordan. This agreement, however, like others of its kind, was observed only in part. For years afterward, the Jewish inhabitants of Jerusalem became the constant targets of sniping attacks and shooting incidents which, over the years, took their toll in lives and material damage.

The Armistice Agreement with Jordan left Israeli Jerusalem encompassed on three sides — north, east and south — by hostile Arab districts, with only its western approaches open to the rest of Israel by way of the winding mountain road linking Jerusalem with the coastal plain to the west. The two parts of the city — the Jordanian and Israeli — were cut off

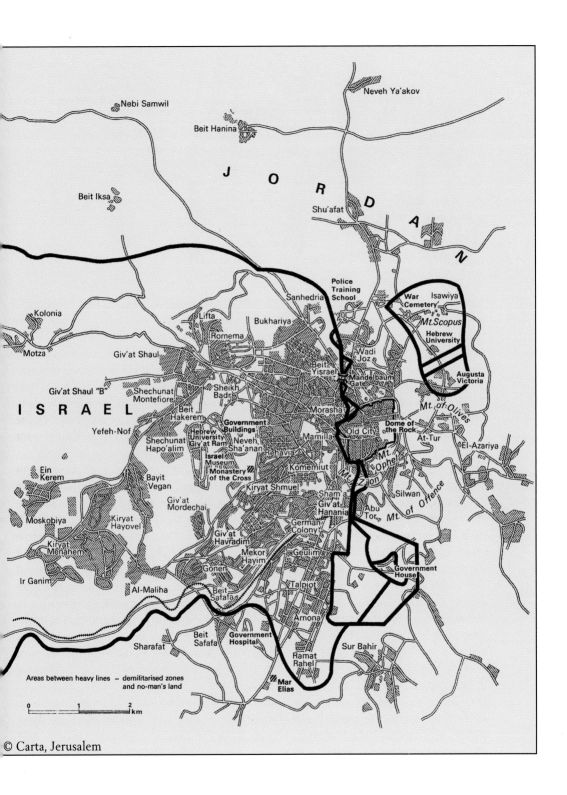

Nebi Samwil

Beit Hanina

Neveh Ya'akov

J O R D A N

Beit Iksa

Shu'afat

Kolonia

Lifta

Sanhedria

Police
Training
School

Bukhariya

War
Cemetery

Isawiya

Mt. Scopus

Romema

Hebrew
University

Motza

Giv'at Shaul

Wadi
Joz

Giv'at Shaul "B"

Shechunat
Montefiore

Sheikh
Badr

Beit
Yisrael

Mandelbaum
Gate

Augusta
Victoria

Yefeh-Nof

Beit
Hakerem

Government
Buildings

Morasha

Mt. of Olives

I S R A E L

Hebrew
University
Giv'at Ram

Neveh
Sha'anan

Mamilla

Old City

Dome of
the Rock

At-Tur

El-Azariya

Shechunat
Hapo'alim

Israel
Museum

Rehavia

Komemiut

Mt.
Ophel

Silwan

Ein
Kerem

Monastery
of the Cross

Kiryat Shmuel

Sham'a

Mt. Zion

Mt. of Offence

Bayit
Vegan

Giv'at
Mordechai

Giv'at
Hanania

Abu
Tor

Moskobiya

Kiryat
Hayovel

German
Colony

Kiryat
Menahem

Giv'at
Havradim

Mekor
Hayim

Geulim

Government
House

Ir Ganim

Gonen

Al-Maliha

Beit
Safafa

Talpiot

Arnona

Sur Bahir

Sharafat

Beit
Safafa

Government
Hospital

Ramat
Rahel

Mar
Elias

Areas between heavy lines – demilitarised zones
and no-man's land

0   1   2
└───┴───┴───┴───┘ km

© Carta, Jerusalem

CONCRETE BARRIERS were erected after the War of Independence between the two parts of the divided city to protect the Jewish inhabitants of Jerusalem against sniper attacks from the Arab side. When the city was reunited after the Six-Day War in 1967, these walls were pulled down.

from each other, with barbed wire and mine-fields preventing all contact. Only members of the Diplomatic Corps and the clergy were permitted to cross the lines freely and non-Jewish tourists were allowed to cross from the Jordanian side to the Israeli side, but not vice versa. All such traffic was funnelled through a single control point — the Mandelbaum Gate. Jordan denied Jews access to the Western Wall (despite its stipulation in the Armistice Agreement) and Israeli Moslems could not visit their shrines in the Old City.

Despite these hardships, Jerusalem, for the third time in its history, became the capital of Israel. The city developed accordingly and new suburbs were built to accomodate refugees from the Old City, new immigrants, survivors of the Nazi holocaust and Jewish refugees from Arab countries.

Next to the newly housed Knesset (Parliament) a complex of Government offices was built. In place of the abandoned Mt. Scopus university and hospital the new Hebrew University campus was built at Giv'at Ram, and the new Hadassah Hospital was located in Ein Kerem. The remains of Theodor Herzl, founder of Zionism, was transferred for burial to Mount Herzl, the venue of many state ceremonies. To the west of Mount Herzl, the Yad Vashem memorial and archive was founded to commemorate the victims of the holocaust.

Despite rapid growth, Israeli Jerusalem suffered the tribulations of a divided city. The borders which enclosed West Jerusalem on three sides allowed for expansion westwards only into an area of mountainous terrain and steep slopes. New neighbourhoods were now far removed from the city's former business and commercial centres to the east. There was little space suitable for big industry so that only light industry began to develop in the Romema and Giv'at Shaul areas. The number of inhabitants did increase but not as much as in the rest of the country and Jerusalem, formerly the second largest city, now dropped to third place.

Little improvement was found in East (Arab) Jerusalem under the rule of the Hashemite Kingdom of Jordan. The population there, at the end of the war of 1948, numbered about 65,000, approximately one-half of them living in the Old City. Nineteen years later, in 1967, the number of people in that part of the city was still under 66,000 — 25,000 of them in the Old City, Indeed, the number of Christians within the overall population had diminished to 10,800.

The main reason for the slow-down in the development of East Jerusalem was to be

MANDELBAUM GATE. The gateway between divided Jerusalem.

found in the official economic policy of the Hashemite Kingdom. The accent was on the development of Jordan's East Bank at the expense of the West Bank, in general, and of Jerusalem, in particular. This policy was coupled with deliberate discrimination against the Christian population. East Jerusalem, too, found itself restricted in the possibilities of its expansion, in effect being able to expand only northward along the road to Ramallah. Building activity increased somewhat also in the vicinity of the American Colony and in the more distant suburbs, such as El-Azariya (Bethany) and Abu Dis. The commercial centre during the Jordanian occupation was Saladin Street, opposite Herod's Gate.

East Jerusalem continued to be a centre for the inhabitants of the West Bank even though the city of Shechem (Nablus) was a growing source of competition. But Jerusalem was the residence of the Moslem courts, numerous Christian institutions, several religious educational institutions, as well as religious and archaeological research institutes. Christian tourism to Christendom's holy places became a major economic factor, with the souvenir industry and the tourist services turning into the chief sources of income in East Jerusalem under the Jordanians.

Divided Jerusalem was visible outwardly too: the two sectors of the city were separated by stretches of no-man's land covered with refuse and junk, mine-fields and rolls of barbed wire, with concrete walls and barriers of various shapes and sizes. In a number of cases the frontier ran between the backyards of houses, or between the houses themselves.

UNITED JERUSALEM
SINCE 1967

Jerusalem was reunited in 1967 in the wake of the Six-Day War. Shortly after the war, all the walls, barriers and obstacles that had blocked off one part of the city from the other were removed, and Jerusalem became one again. Jews returned to the Jewish Quarter and were once again able to visit the Western Wall and the Temple Mount. Moslems and Christians were assured free access to their sacred sites.

Reunification led to an immediate improvement in municipal services such as sanitation and water supply for the eastern sections of the city. Previously blocked streets were repaired and opened to traffic, and split neighbourhoods were brought together again. Mounds of garbage and rubbish that had accumulated at the foot of the Old City walls were cleared, to be replaced by a 'green belt' that adorned the walls around the entire circumference of the Old City. From north to south, the old signs of division were obliterated and the ravages of war repaired and made good. Building activity in the city experienced an unprecedented boom, and Jerusalem took on a different appearance. New Jewish neighbourhoods were created with housing projects on the hills surrounding the city, while modern Arab areas like Wadi Joz and Shu'afat launched programmes of expansion. The Hebrew University campus on Mount Scopus was rebuilt, as was the nearby Hadassah Hospital complex, to serve all of the city's inhabitants, Jews and Arabs.

Reunification gave Jerusalem a new lease on life. No longer a cul-de-sac hemmed in on three sides, the city had regained its natural place as the capital and geographical centre of the country, with major traffic arteries leading in all directions. Once again, Jerusalem was able to expand and develop, and indeed did so.

Reunification signified yet another important change: almost overnight, it transformed Jerusalem into a major focus of archaeological exploration, mainly in the Old City, hitherto inaccessible to the Israeli archaeologist. Of particular interest is the combined task of uncovering the secrets of Jerusalem's past and restoring its antiquities, while carefully rebuilding the Jewish Quarter. Our store of knowledge concerning the past has been immeasurably enriched by this effort.

Special credit is due to Teddy Kollek, the legendary six-term mayor of Jerusalem, who had already been at the helm of Israel's capital for two years. At the time he found himself face to face with a historic opportunity of monumental proportions, caused by yet another upheaval in the checkered history of this tortured city. Kollek seized the moment. A man of vision, but even more a master of action, Kollek promptly embarked on the most ambitious bulding project since the days of Herod. Indeed, looking at the Jerusalem he passed on to his successors, one is tempted to say that Kollek surpassed Herod in beautifying this city that means so much to so many.

..... Municipal boundary of East Jerusalem May 1967
⊥⊥⊥ Proposed master plan for boundary of East Jerusalem, May 1967
──── Armistice line, 1949–1967
──── West Jerusalem (ISRAEL) municipal boundary
━━━━ Municipal boundary of united Jerusalem 28.6.1967

© Carta, Jerusalem

0 500 1000
     m

INDEX

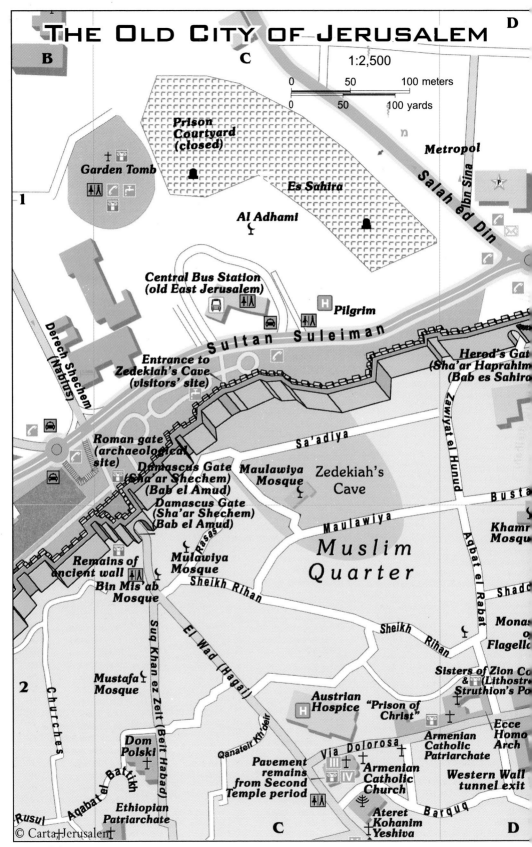

THE OLD CITY OF JERUSALEM

B

C

D

1:2,500

0   50   100 meters

0   50   100 yards

Prison Courtyard (closed)

Garden Tomb

Metropol

Es Sahira

Salah ed Din

Ibn Sina

Al Adhami

1

Central Bus Station (old East Jerusalem)

H Pilgrim

Sultan Suleiman

Herod's Gat (Sha'ar Haprahim (Bab es Sahira

Entrance to Zedekiah's Cave (visitors' site)

Derech Shechem (Nablus)

Zawiyat el Hunud

Sa'adiya

Roman gate (archaeological site)

Damascus Gate (Sha'ar Shechem) (Bab el Amud)

Maulawiya Mosque

Zedekiah's Cave

Busta

Damascus Gate (Sha'ar Shechem) (Bab el Amud)

Maulawiya

Khamr Mosqu

Rasas

Remains of ancient wall

Mulawiya Mosque

Bin Mis'ab Mosque

Sheikh Rihan

M u s l i m
Q u a r t e r

Aqbat el Rabat

Shadc

Monas o Flagello

Sheikh Rihan

2

Churches

Mustafa Mosque

Suq Khan ez Zeit (Beit Habad)

El Wad (Hagai)

Austrian Hospice H

"Prison of Christ"

Sisters of Zion Co & (Lithostr Struthion's Po

Dom Polski

Qanateir Khidelr

Via Dolorosa

Armenian Catholic Patriarchate

Ecce Homo Arch

Aqabat el Battikh

Pavement remains from Second Temple period

III
IV

Armenian Catholic Church

Western Wall tunnel exit

Rusul

Ethiopian Patriarchate

Ateret Kohanim Yeshiva

Barquq

© Carta, Jerusalem

C

D

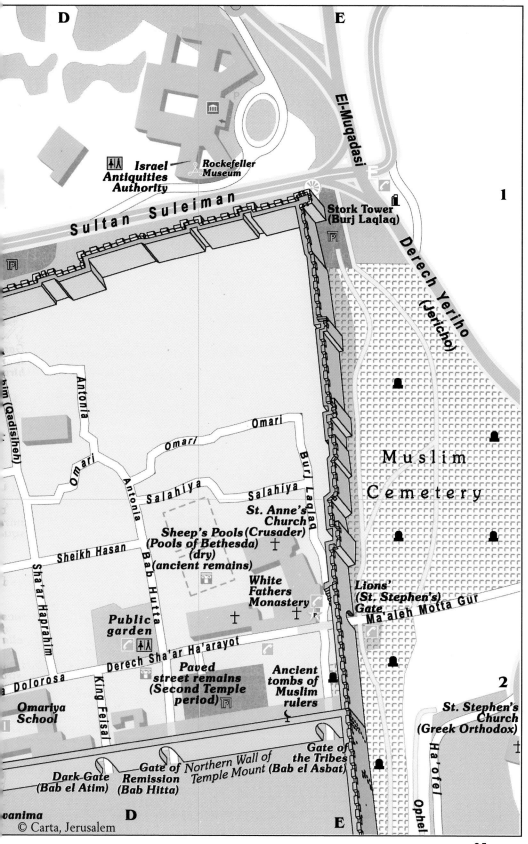

D

E

Israel
Antiquities
Authority

Rockefeller
Museum

El-Muqadasi

1

Sultan Suleiman

Stork Tower
(Burj Laqlaq)

Derech Yeriho
(Jericho)

Antonia

Omari (Qadisheh)

Omari

Omari

Omari

Salahiya

Salahiya

Muslim
Cemetery

Antonia

Burj Laqlaq

St. Anne's
Church
(Crusader)

Sheep's Pools
(Pools of Bethesda)
(dry)
(ancient remains)

Sheikh Hasan

Bab Hutta

White
Fathers
Monastery

Lions'
(St. Stephen's)
Gate

Ma'aleh Motta Gur

Public
garden

Sha'ar Haprahim

Dolorosa

Derech Sha'ar Ha'arayot

King Feisal

Paved
street remains
(Second Temple
period)

Ancient
tombs of
Muslim
rulers

2

St. Stephen's
Church
(Greek Orthodox)

Omariya
School

Ha'ofel

Ophel

Dark Gate
(Bab el Atim)

Gate of
Remission
(Bab Hitta)

Gate of Northern Wall of
Temple Mount (Bab el Asbat)

Gate of
the Tribes

vanima

D

E

© Carta, Jerusalem

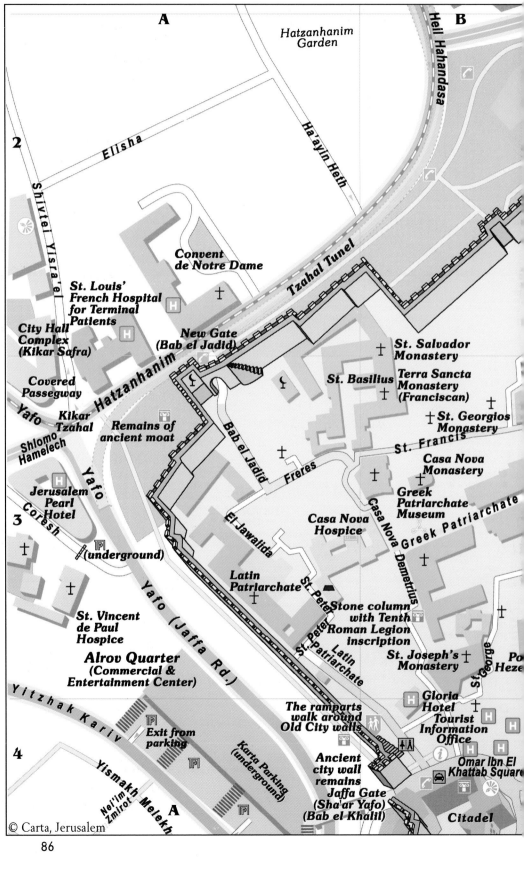

A

Hatzanhanim Garden

B

Hell Hahandasa

Elisha

2

Ha'ayin Heth

Shivtei Yisra'el

Tzahal Tunel

Convent de Notre Dame

St. Louis' French Hospital for Terminal Patients

St. Salvador Monastery

City Hall Complex (Kikar Safra)

New Gate (Bab el Jadid)

Terra Sancta Monastery (Franciscan)

St. Basilius

Covered Passegway

Hatzanhanim

St. Georgios Monastery

Yafo

Kikar Tzahal

Remains of ancient moat

Bab el Jadid

St. Francis

Shlomo Hamelech

Casa Nova Monastery

Freres

Greek Patriarchate Museum

Jerusalem Pearl Hotel

Casa Nova Hospice

Casa Nova Demetrius

Greek Patriarchate

Coresh

3

El Jawalida

(underground)

Latin Patriarchate

St. Peter

St. Vincent de Paul Hospice

Stone column with Tenth Roman Legion inscription

Alrov Quarter (Commercial & Entertainment Center)

Yafo (Jaffa Rd.)

St. Peter Latin Patriarchate

St. Joseph's Monastery

St. George

Po Heze

Yitzhak Kariv

Gloria Hotel

The ramparts walk around Old City walls

Tourist Information Office

Exit from parking

4

Karta Parking (underground)

Ancient city wall remains

Omar Ibn El Khattab Square

Yismakh Melekh

Jaffa Gate (Sha'ar Yafo) (Bab el Khalil)

Citadel

Nei'im Zmirot

A

© Carta, Jerusalem

86

B

Damascus Gate
(Sha'ar Shechem)
(Bab el Amud)

C

Maulawiya

D

Aqbat el Rabat

Remains of
ancient wall

Mulawiya
Mosque

Muslim
Quarter

Bin Mis'ab
Mosque

Sheikh Rihan

El Wad (Hagai)

Sheikh Rihan

2

Mustafa
Mosque

Suq Khan ez Zeit (Beit Habad)

Austrian
Hospice

"Prison of
Christ"

Armenian
Catholic
Patriarchate

Dom
Polski

Qanateir Kh'deir

Via Dolorosa

Armenian
Catholic
Church

adon's
astery

Ethiopian
Patriarchate

Pavement
remains
from Second
Temple period

Ateret
Kohanim
Yeshiva

Barquq

Aqabat el Battikh

Er Rusul

Alliance

St. Catherine's
Monastery

VII

Via Dolorosa

V

El Wad (Hagai)

Hazon
Yehezkel
Yeshiva

hanqa
osque

El Khanqa

VIII

Coptic
Patriarchate
(Station IX)

St. Veronica

German
Hostel

VI

Hamidrasha   Aqabat et Takiya (Khiski Sultan)

Crusader
Gate
(closed)

IX

Church of
the Holy Sepulchre
(Stations X-XIV)

X-XIV

Ethiopian
Monastery
St.
Abraham's
Monastery

Church
of Alexander
Nievsky

El Wad (Hagai)

3

hristian
uarter

St. Helena

Remains
of Roman
paved street

Church of the
Redeemer
& lookout
tower

Aqabat es Saraya

Torat
Hakohanim
Yeshiva

P

El Qirami

Muristan

Market

Kolel
Galicia

Khaldiya

El Wad (Hagai)

Aftimos

Monument
to Knights
of St. John

Market Place
Promenade

Shuvu Banim
(Hayei Olam)
Yeshiva

Church
of St. John
the Baptist

Khan
es Sultan

Model of
Jerusalem
in First Temple
period

David

St. Mark

Entrance
Market
Prom-
enade

Israelite tower
(archaeological
site)

Bab el Silsila (Hashalshet)

Rahel Yanait
Ben Zvi Youth
Center

4

ronite
nvent

B

Roof
Prom-
enade

Mughrabi
Synagogue

Genesis
Jerusalem
Institute

C

Jewish   Quarter

D

Shonei Halakhot

arta, Jerusalem

Ethiopian Patriarchate

Ateret Kohanim Yeshiva

Bani Ghawanim Gate

D

VII

Via Dolorosa

V

El Wad (Hagai)

Hazon Yehezkel Yeshiva

Inspecto Gate (Bab en Nadhir)

St. Veronica

VI

Coptic Patriarchate (Station IX)

German Hostel

Alla ed Din

IX

Hamidrasha Aqabat et Takiya (Khiski Sultan)

"Hakotel Hakatan" (Little Western Wall)

Iron Ga (Bab el Hadid

3

Church of Alexander Nievsky

Aqabat es Saraya

Iron Gate

El Wad (Hagai)

Cotto Merce Gate (Bab Qatt

Ethiopian Monastery St. Abraham's Monastery

Torat Hakohanim Yeshiva

Suq el Qattanin (Cotton Merchants Market)

Purific Gate

Church of the Redeemer & lookout tower

Kolel Galicia

El Qirami

Khaldiya

Shuvu Banim (Hayei Olam) Yeshiva

Mah'khama

Covered passageway

Go of Ch (B S

Muristan

Market Place Promenade

El Hakkari

El Wad (Hagai)

Sharsheret Hadorot Center

Suq el Lahhamim

Suq el Attarin

Suq el Khawalat

Khan es Sultan

Model of Jerusalem in First Temple period

Bab el Silsila (Hashalshelet)

Wilson's Arch

Western Wall Tunnels (entrance)

Western Wall of Temple Mount

Lahhamim

Entrance Market Prom- enade

Israelite tower (archaeological site)

Rahel Yanait Ben Zvi Youth Center

Hakotel

Mughrabi Gate (Bab el Maghariba

Roof Prom- enade

Mughrabi Synagogue

Genesis Jerusalem Institute

Shonei Halakhot

Jewish Quarter

Habad Cardo

Quarter (Hayehudim) (covered passageway)

4

"Alone on the Walls" Exhibit

"Broad Wall" Wall remains from First Temple period

Ha-Omer

Bonei Ha-Homa

Ha-Meshorerim

Ha-Shoarim

Misgav Ladach

Temple Institute and Museum of Temple vessels

Western Wall Entrance & Exit

Seconda street remains

Telem

"Burnt House" (archaeological site)

Robins A

Cardo

Tiferet Israel

Reconstruction of Temple menorah

Ma'aleh Shlomo Goren

Davic Cen

Hurva Square

Ha-Karaim

Hakotel Yeshiva

Sidna Omar

Hurva Synagogue

Ramban Synagogue

Herodian Mansions (archaeological site)

Misgav Ladach

Porat Yosef Yeshiva

Dung Gate

Four Sephardic synagogues

Hayye Olam

Model of Holy Temple

Jewish Quarter

Nevel

Byzantine Cardo Sapir Center

Barkai

Monument to the Fallen in War of Independence

Ha-Tupim

Rothschild House and Batei Mahasse Square

Nea Church (closed to public)

Galiled

Beit Ha-Shoeva

Misgav Ladach Hashmonit

Nahman

Batei Mahasse

Tanners Gate

Dung Gate

Ha-Shalom

5

C

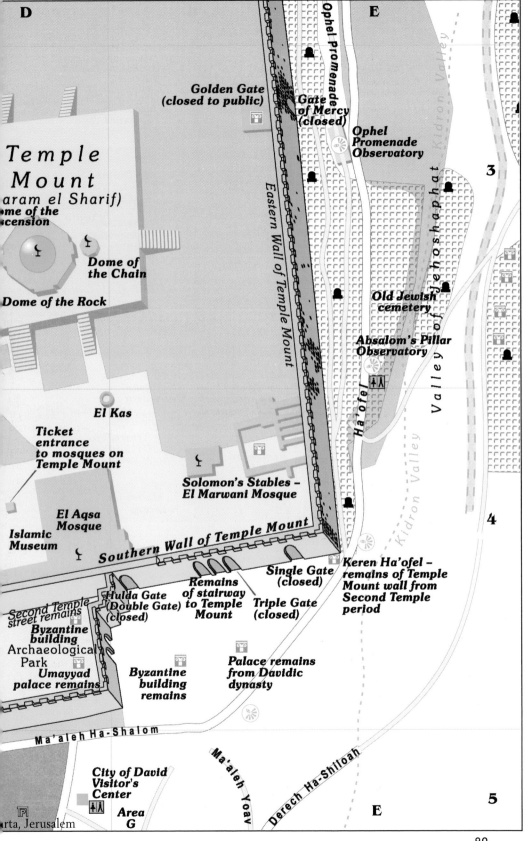

D

E

Temple Mount
(Ḥaram el Sharif)

Dome of the Ascension

Golden Gate
(closed to public)

Gate of Mercy
(closed)

Ophel Promenade

Ophel Promenade Observatory

ए *Dome of the Chain*

Dome of the Rock

3

Eastern Wall of Temple Mount

Kidron Valley

Old Jewish cemetery

Valley of Jehoshaphat

Absalom's Pillar Observatory

El Kas

Ticket entrance to mosques on Temple Mount

Ha'ofel

Kidron Valley

Solomon's Stables – El Marwani Mosque

4

El Aqsa Mosque

Islamic Museum

Southern Wall of Temple Mount

Kidron Valley

Keren Ha'ofel – remains of Temple Mount wall from Second Temple period

Single Gate (closed)

Remains of stairway to Temple Mount

Hulda Gate (Double Gate) (closed)

Triple Gate (closed)

Second Temple street remains

Byzantine building

Archaeological Park

Umayyad palace remains

Byzantine building remains

Palace remains from Davidic dynasty

Ma'aleh Ha-Shalom

Ma'aleh Yoav

Derech Ha-Shiloah

E

5

City of David Visitor's Center

Area G

arta, Jerusalem

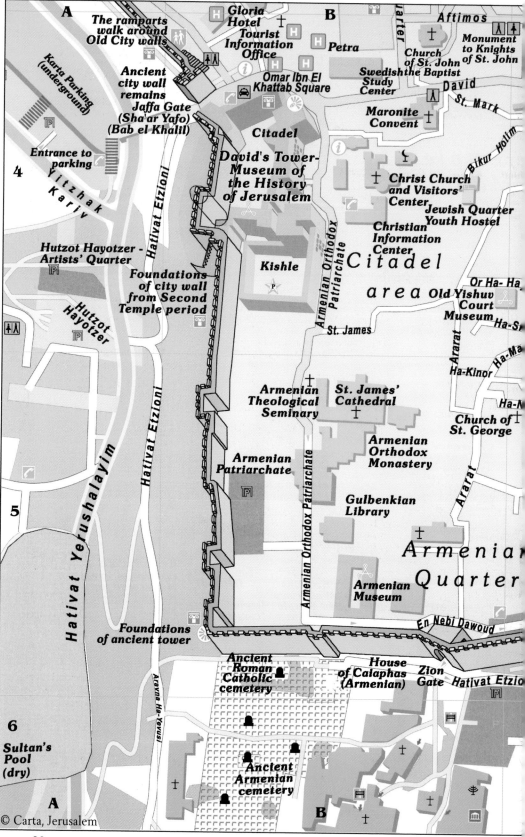

The ramparts walk around Old City walls

Gloria Hotel

Tourist Information Office

Petra

Aftimos

Monument to Knights of St. John

Church of St. John the Baptist

Swedish Study Center

Maronite Convent

David

St. Mark

Ancient city wall remains

Jaffa Gate (Sha'ar Yafo) (Bab el Khalil)

Omar Ibn El Khattab Square

Citadel

Christ Church and Visitors' Center

Jewish Quarter Youth Hostel

Christian Information Center

Bikur Holim

Karta Parking (underground)

Entrance to parking

David's Tower-Museum of the History of Jerusalem

Citadel area

Old Yishuv Court Museum

Or Ha- Ha

Ha-S

4

Yitzhak Kariv

Hativat Etzioni

Kishle

Armenian Orthodox Patriarchate

St. James

Ararat

Ha-Ma

Ha-Kinor

Hutzot Hayotzer - Artists' Quarter

Foundations of city wall from Second Temple period

Ha-N

Hutzot Hayotzer

Armenian Theological Seminary

St. James' Cathedral

Church of St. George

Armenian Patriarchate

Armenian Orthodox Monastery

5

Hativat Yerushalayim

Hativat Etzioni

Armenian Orthodox Patriarchate

Gulbenkian Library

Ararat

Armenian

Quarter

Armenian Museum

Foundations of ancient tower

En Nebi Dawoud

Arayha Ha-Yevusi

Ancient Roman Catholic cemetery

House of Caiaphas (Armenian)

Zion Gate

Hativat Etzio

6

Sultan's Pool (dry)

Ancient Armenian cemetery

A

B

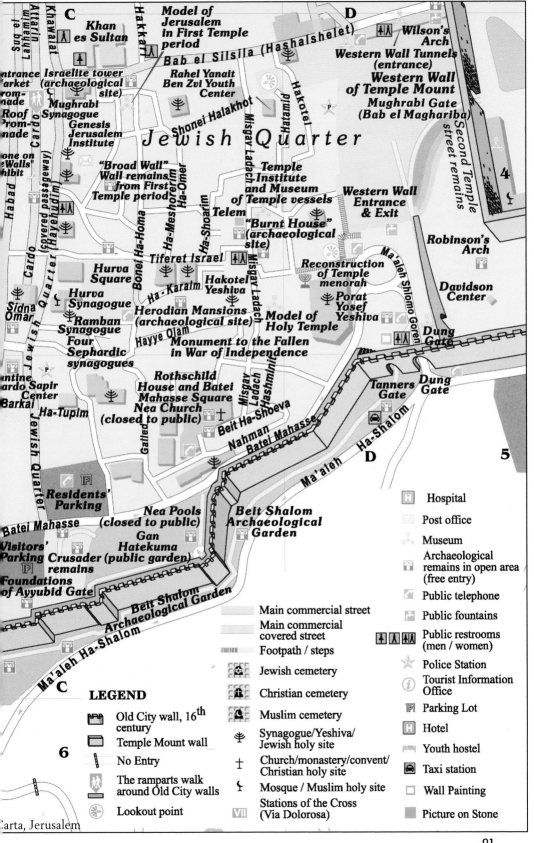

C Khan es Sultan

Model of Jerusalem in First Temple period

D Wilson's Arch

Bab el Silsila (Hashalshelet)

Western Wall Tunnels (entrance)

Israelite tower (archaeological site)

Rahel Yanait Ben Zvi Youth Center

Western Wall of Temple Mount

Mughrabi Gate (Bab el Maghariba)

Entrance Market Promenade

Roof Promenade

Mughrabi Synagogue Genesis Jerusalem Institute

Shonei Halakhot

Hakotel

Misgav Ladach

Second Temple street remains

Jewish Quarter

Stone on the Walls Exhibit

"Broad Wall" Wall remains from First Temple period

Ha-Omer

Ha-Meshorerim

Temple Institute and Museum of Temple vessels

Western Wall Entrance & Exit

4

Habad

Cardo (covered passageway) (Hayehudim)

Telem

Ha-Shoarim

"Burnt House" (archaeological site)

Robinson's Arch

Tiferet Israel

Misgav Ladach

Reconstruction of Temple menorah

Cardo

Hurva Square

Bonei Ha-Homa

Hakotel Yeshiva

Davidson Center

Hurva Synagogue

Ha-Karaim

Herodian Mansions (archaeological site)

Porat Yosef Yeshiva

Ma'aleh Shlomo Goren

Sidna Omar

Ramban Synagogue

Model of Holy Temple

Dung Gate

Four Sephardic synagogues

Hayye Olam

Monument to the Fallen in War of Independence

Byzantine Cardo Sapir Center

Barkai

Ha-Tupim

Rothschild House and Batei Mahasse Square

Misgav Ladach Hashmlni

Tanners Gate

Dung Gate

Jewish Quarter

Nea Church (closed to public)

Beit Ha-Shoeva

Nahman

Batei Mahasse

Ma'aleh Ha-Shalom

D

5

Residents' Parking

Nea Pools (closed to public)

Beit Shalom Archaeological Garden

Batei Mahasse

Gan Hatekuma

Visitors' Parking Crusader remains (public garden)

Foundations of Ayyubid Gate

Beit Shalom Archaeological Garden

Ma'aleh Ha-Shalom

C

LEGEND

6

Main commercial street	
Main commercial covered street	
Footpath / steps	
Jewish cemetery	
Christian cemetery	
Muslim cemetery	
Synagogue/Yeshiva/ Jewish holy site	
Church/monastery/convent/ Christian holy site	
Mosque / Muslim holy site	
Stations of the Cross (Via Dolorosa)	VII

Old City wall, 16th century

Temple Mount wall

No Entry

The ramparts walk around Old City walls

Lookout point

Hospital	
Post office	
Museum	
Archaeological remains in open area (free entry)	
Public telephone	
Public fountains	
Public restrooms (men / women)	
Police Station	
Tourist Information Office	
Parking Lot	
Hotel	
Youth hostel	
Taxi station	
Wall Painting	
Picture on Stone	

Carta, Jerusalem

The Old City - Sites & Institutions

A
Absalom's Pillar observatory E3
Alrov Quarter (Commercial & Entertainment Center) A3
Ancient moat (remains) A3
Ancient wall (remains) C2
Armenian Catholic Ch. C2
Armenian Mus. B5
Armenian Orthodox Mon. B5
Armenian Patr. B5
Armenian Theological Sem. B5
Armenian Quarter B-C5
Ashkenazi Syn. Yemin Moshe A5
Ateret Kohanim Yeshiva C2
Austrian Hospice C2
Ayyubid Gate (foundations) C5

B
Bab el Amud (Gate) B-C 1-2
Bab el Asbat (Gate) E2
Bab el Atim (Gate) D2
Bab el Hadid (Gate) D3
Bab el Jadid (New Gate) A2
Bab el Khalil A-B4
Bab el Maghariba D4
Bab el Qattanim (Gate) D3
Bab en Nadhir (Gate) D3
Bab es Sahira D1
Bab es Silsila (Gate) D3
Bab Hitta (Gate) D2
Bani Ghawanima Gate D2
Barclay's Gate D4
Batei Mahasse Square C5
Beit Shalom Archeological Garden C5
Broad Wall (arch.) C4
Burj Laqlaq (Tower) E1
Burnt House (arch.) C4
Byzantine building remains D4

C
Cardo (ancient Byzantine street) C4
Casa Nova Hospice A-B3
Casa Nova Mon. B3
Central Bus Station (Old) C1
Christ Church and Visitor's Center B4
Christian Information Cen. B4
Christian Quarter B3
Ch. of the Holy Sepulchre (Stations X-XIV) B3
Ch. of the Redeemer C3
Citadel (Tower of David) B4
City Hall Complex A2
City of David (Ancient Jerusalem) D-E5
City of David Visitor's Center D5

City wall (remains) A4
Convent de Notre Dame A2
Coptic Patr. (Station IX) C3
Cotton Merchants Gate D3
Cotton Merchants Market D3

D
Damascus Gate B-C 1-2
Dark Gate D2
Davidic Dynasty Palace E4
David's Village A4
Davidson Center D4
Dom Polski C2
Dome of the Ascension D3
Dome of the Chain D-E3
Dome of the Rock D3
Double Gate E4
Dung Gate D5

E
Eastern Wall E3
Ecce Homo Arch D2
El Aqsa Mosque D4
El Kas - (feet washing) D-E4
Ethiopian Patr. C2

F
First Temple Wall (remains) C4
Four Sephardic synagogues C5

G
Gan Hatekuma (garden) C5
Garden Tomb B-C1
Gate of Mercy (closed) E3
Gate of Remission D2
Gate of the Chain D3
Gate of the Tribes E2
Genesis Jerusalem Institute C3
German Hostel C3
Gihon Spring E5
Gloria Hotel B3-4
Golden Gate (closed) E3
Greek Patr. Mus. B3
Gulbenkian Library B5

H
Hakotel Hakatan (Little Western Wall) D3
Haram el Sharif D3
Herod's Gate (Bab es Sahira) (Sha'ar Haprahim) D1
Herodian Mansions (arch.) C4
Hezekiah's Tunnel E5
History of Jerusalem Mus. (Tower of David) B4
House of Caiaphas B5
Hulda Gate E4
Hurva Square C4
Hurva Syn. (ruin) C4
Hutzot Hayotzer - Artists' Quarter A4

I
Inspector Gate D3
Iron Gate D3

Islamic Mus. D4
Israel Antiquities Authority D-E1
Israelite tower (arch.) C4

J
Jaffa Gate (Sha'ar Yafo) A-B4
Jerusalem Archaeological Park E4
Jerusalem Holy Temple Model D4
Jewish Quarter C-D4

K
Keren Ha'ofel (remains) E4
Kfar David A4
Kidron Valley E4
Kikar Safra A2-3
Kishle - police station B4

L
Lions' (St. Stephen's) Gate E2
Lithostrotos C-D2
Little Western Wall D3

M
Market (Peddlar's) B2
Market Place Promenade C3
Maronite Convent B4
Mon. of the Flagellation D2
Montefiore's Windmill A5
Monument to Fallen in War of Independence C-D 4-5
Muslim Quarter C-D2
Mughrabi Gate (Bab el Magharib) D4
Muristan B3
Muslim Cem. E1-2
Muslim rulers' tombs E2

N
Nea Ch. (mosaic) C5
Nea Pools (arch.) C5
New Gate (Bab el Jadid) A2
Notre Dame Hotel A2

O
Old City - Res. Parking C5
Old City Ramparts A-B4
Old Yishuv Court Museum B4
One Last Day Museum (War of Independence) C4
Ophel Promenade & Observatory E2-3

P
Pninat Dan Hotel A3
Police station D4
Pools of Bethesda D-E2
Pool of Hezekiah B3-4
Porat Yosef Yeshiva D4
Prison of Christ C-D2
Purification Gate D3

R
Rahel Yana'it Ben Zvi Youth Center C4
Ramban Syn. C4
Robinson's Arch D4
Rockefeller Mus. D-E1
Roman Cath. Cem. (arch.) B5

Roman gate (arch.) C1
Rothschild House C5

S
Saint Anne's Ch. (Crusader) E2
Saint John the Baptist Ch. B4
Saint Louis Hospital A2
Sapir Center C5
Second Temple city wall (foundations) A-B4
Second Temple street D4
Sephardic Syn. (Yemin Moshe) A5
Sheep's Pools of Bethesda D-E2
Single Gate E4
Sisters of Zion Convent C-D2
Solomon's Stables E4
Stairway to Temple Mount (Remains) E4
Stork Tower E1
Struthion's Pools C-D2
Suq el Qattanim (Cotton Merchants Market) D3

T
Tanners Gate D5
Telem, Visitor and tourist center for people with disabilities and special needs D5
Temple Institute and Museum of Temple Vessels C-D4
Temple Menorah reconstr. C4
Temple Model D4
Temple Mount D3
Tenth Roman Legion stone column inscription B3
Tourist Information Office B4
Tourist Police E2
Tower of David B4
Triple Gate E4

U
Umayyad palace remains D4

W
Walkway on Old City walls (ascent & descent) A-B4
Western Wall (Wailing Wall) D4
Western Wall tunnels D4
Wilson's Arch D4

Y
Yemin Moshe A5

Z
Zedekiah's Cave C1
Zion Gate B5
Zionist Confederation House A5